Betty Crocker's
NEW
DINNER for TWO
COOKBOOK

Illustrated by Margaret Fleming and Jean Simpson

GOLDEN PRESS · NEW YORK
WESTERN PUBLISHING COMPANY, INC.

Thirteenth Printing, 1972

Dear Friend,

If you are a bride, a business girl, career wife, or a mother whose children are away from home — this book is for you.

The *New Dinner for Two Cook Book* takes you on a grand tour through pages of exciting menus, recipes, tips, and ideas for planning and preparing different and delicious dinners for two.

Here you will find recipes that make the most of your time, your food budget, and your creativity as a cook with specialties of every region and season and wonderful meals to serve on many occasions.

And when you entertain, turn to "When Company Comes" or simply double the recipes for two from other pages.

We hope that you "small-home-makers" everywhere, and those who cook for one, will enjoy the *New Dinner for Two* and its friendly fare — favorite, fancy, and family style.

Sincerely,

Betty Crocker

P.S. Every recipe and menu in this book has been tested for you, both in our kitchens at General Mills and in homes like yours across the country.

Contents

Seven-Day Sampler

Dinner for two can be an exciting adventure every day in the week when you choose tempting menus from any chapter of this book. Here is a Seven-Day Sampler of model dinners for two to start you on your way. Remember, good menus begin with these few simple rules.

1. Look at each day as a whole! Consider your breakfast and lunch when you plan your dinner menu.

2. Contrast strong flavors with bland ones, remembering that too many pronounced and different tastes cancel one another out.

3. Serve some soft, some solid, some crisp, and some creamy foods in the same menu.

4. Have both cold and hot foods; even in summer plan one hot dish for dinner. Sometimes serve sherbet with a roast, chilled relish with fowl.

5. Serve tart or spicy foods early in the meal to stimulate the appetite; serve sweets last to deaden it.

6. Season food sparingly—just enough to bring out the natural flavors.

7. End a heavy, rich meal with a tart fruit, a light dessert, or a highly flavored cheese to speed up digestion.

8. Remember that the sight of food is stimulating to the appetite—be an artist in your choice.

- *Serve foods that contrast in color.*
- *Avoid all round or all long-shaped pieces of food on plate.*
- *Serve foods cut in varying sizes.*

9. Serve hot foods really hot and cold foods thoroughly chilled. Garnish them simply with colorful fruits, vegetables, or greens that are equally good to eat.

When Time Counts

Timing is a very important part of meal preparation, and one of the most difficult to master. To bring all dishes on the menu to the table at the proper time, each at the perfect temperature and degree of doneness, is an accomplishment requiring planning, practice, and concentration.

Here are some "dos" and a few "don'ts" for arriving serenely at your own dinner table with the meat beautifully brown, hot and tender, the salad crisp, cold and dewy, the rolls fragrantly fresh from the oven, and every little garnish prettily in place.

• List the order in which you plan to prepare food for the meal. First read through your recipes, noting cooking times and estimating pre-cooking preparation time. Then make a rough time schedule to follow.

• Wash and prepare fresh vegetables and salad greens as soon as you return from the market, before storing them. This will save you many minutes at dinnertime and will also result in crisper, tastier salads because the ingredients will be thoroughly dry and chilled when you use them.

• Make salad dressings sometimes in quantity and keep refrigerated; keep a covered jar of seasoned flour on the shelf for gravies and breading meat and fish.

• Make refrigerator desserts and molded salads the night before or early in the day.

• Have water and coffee measured and ready beforehand.

• Plan to set the table, make the dessert, and prepare vegetables and relishes after you finish the breakfast dishes to cut down on work later in the day, when your energy is often lower.

• Avoid planning too many new dishes for any one meal; doing the unfamiliar always requires more time.

• Avoid leaving too many tasks for the last minute. Making gravy, salad, and coffee and warming rolls in the oven all at once can be confusing.

• Keep shears or scissors in the kitchen and use them to snip fruits, celery, meat, chicken, and dozens of other ingredients that require more time to chop.

• Use your thermometer and kitchen timer.

• Assemble all ingredients and utensils on a tray before you begin to bake. This saves many minutes of actual preparation time.

• Set out all serving dishes conveniently on counter or table to speed up last minute serving.

• Clear as you work, wash cooking equipment or put it to soak in water as you finish with each piece. This cuts cleanup time later.

• Keep a list in the kitchen and note each staple item as you use the last of it. Add this to your shopping list at marketing time.

Sunday

Start the week with the cherished custom of Sunday dinner. In the relaxed atmosphere of the day, you can enjoy cooking to perfection the "Best-Liked Dinners" on our list of Favorite American Fare.

*Easy Oven-fried Chicken
Mashed Potatoes (p. 36)
Pan Gravy (p. 121)
Cranberry-Orange Relish
Buttered Green Peas
Strawberry Shortcake*

Schedule for Dinner on Time

Ahead of time:
Make Cranberry-Orange Relish.
Prepare strawberries or start thawing.
Prepare shortcakes.

1 hr. ahead:
Start chicken.

45 min. ahead:
Pare potatoes; start cooking.
Set table.

30 min. ahead:
Shell peas.
Turn chicken.

15 min. ahead:
Start cooking peas.
Make gravy.
Mash potatoes.

Easy Oven-fried Chicken

¼ cup shortening   1 frying chicken (2 to
  (part butter)   2½ lb.), quartered
Seasoned Flour (right)

Heat oven to 425° (hot). Melt the fat in a shallow baking pan in oven. Wash and dry chicken.

Place Seasoned Flour in paper sack. Drop in a quarter of chicken at a time. Flour chicken by shaking sack, holding it closed with hand. Arrange floured chicken skin-side-down in baking pan in single layer. Bake 45 min. Turn skin-side-up and continue baking about 15 min., until tender. Serve hot with Pan Gravy (p. 121). *2 generous servings.*

Seasoned Flour

½ cup all-purpose flour   ¼ tsp. pepper
1 tsp. salt   ¼ tsp. paprika

Pan-fried Chicken

Coat quartered 2- to 2½-lb. frying chicken by shaking in sack containing Seasoned Flour (above). Place in heavy skillet in ½" hot fat. Turn to brown evenly, 15 to 20 min. Add 3 tbsp. water; cover and cook over low heat on top of range 45 to 60 min., or until tender. Uncover last 5 to 10 min. to recrisp. *2 generous servings.*

Cranberry-Orange Relish

½ large or 1 small   2 cups raw or thawed
  unpeeled orange   frozen cranberries
                  1 cup sugar

Put orange and cranberries through food chopper. Mix in sugar and let stand for several hours. Store in a covered jar in refrigerator. *Makes 1½ cups.*

To save time, use frozen Cranberry-Orange Relish —available in many markets.

Buttered Green Peas

You'll need 1½ lb. unshelled fresh peas (makes 1 cup shelled). Shell just before cooking. Cook peas (with a few pods for flavor) in ½ to 1" boiling salted water for 8 to 12 min. Season with butter, salt, and pepper. *2 servings.*

To save time, use 1 pkg. (10 oz.) frozen peas. Follow pkg. directions.

Strawberry Shortcake

Wash and halve 1 to 1½ cups fresh strawberries; sweeten with ⅓ to ½ cup sugar. Let stand 1 hr. at room temperature. Or thaw 1 pkg. (10 oz.) frozen strawberries. Make Shortcakes (p. 73). Split Shortcakes; fill and top with fruit. Serve with whipped cream or coffee cream. *2 servings.*

Monday

If Monday is busy and hectic, treat yourself to an easy "Hurry-Up Dinner." The time you save in preparation can be spent in catching up with the day's news and relaxing for a restful hour over coffee.

Pineapple Burgers
Poppy Seed Noodles
Lettuce Wedges
with Mayonnaise Dressing
Hard-crusted Herb-buttered Rolls
Vanilla Ice Cream with Caramel Sauce

Pineapple Burgers

2 pineapple spears or rings	½ lb. ground beef Spicy Sauce (below)

Drain pineapple well. If using pineapple spears, divide meat into 2 patties; form around spears. If using pineapple rings, divide meat into 4 thinner patties; place a ring between two patties, sealing edges. Place burgers on rack 6″ away from broiler unit; broil 5 min. Turn; broil 5 min. more. Pour Spicy Sauce over burgers; serve at once. *2 servings.*

Spicy Sauce: Blend ½ cup brown sugar, ½ cup catsup, and 2 tbsp. prepared mustard in saucepan. Simmer 2 to 3 min.

Poppy Seed Noodles

Cook 2 to 3 oz. noodles (about 1 cup) in 6 cups boiling salted water (1½ tsp. salt). Drain. Add 2 tbsp. butter and 1 tsp. poppy seeds. Stir gently. *2 generous servings.*

Mayonnaise Dressing

Stir 2 tbsp. commercial sour cream into ¼ cup mayonnaise. Season with salt and pepper to taste.

Hard-crusted Herb-buttered Rolls

Split hard-crusted rolls (or other favorite rolls) in half lengthwise. Spread with Herb Butter (right); reassemble; wrap in aluminum foil. Heat in oven.

Herb Butter

¼ cup butter	¼ tsp. each dried
⅛ tsp. ground sage	tarragon, sweet basil, and thyme leaves

Mix all ingredients together.

Caramel Sauce

½ pkg. (14.3-oz. size) golden caramel frosting mix	1 tbsp. light corn syrup 1½ tbsp. butter ⅓ cup milk

Combine frosting mix, corn syrup, and butter in top of double boiler. Add milk gradually. Heat over rapidly boiling water 5 min., stirring occasionally. Store leftover sauce covered in refrigerator. *Makes 1 cup.*

Note: To use half a package, measure entire contents of package and divide in half.

Tuesday

Make Tuesday a Party-for-Two night by trying a company meal. Dinner will have a festive air, whether you're celebrating an important event or just the pleasure of being at home together.

Breaded Veal Chops
Double-deck Potatoes and Carrots
Orange-Bermuda Onion Salad
with Ruby Red Dressing
Whole Wheat Bread
Vanilla Custard Pudding

Breaded Veal Chops

2 loin or rib veal chops, about 1" thick	fine dry bread or cracker crumbs
flour	2 tbsp. fat
1 egg, beaten with 1 tbsp. water	salt and pepper
	¼ cup water or cream

Dip chops in flour, then in beaten egg, then in crumbs. Brown slowly on both sides in hot fat, seasoning with salt and pepper. Pour off excess fat; add water; cover tightly. Simmer 45 to 60 min., or until tender. (It may be necessary to add more liquid from time to time.) Garnish with lemon wedges and stuffed green olives in nest of parsley. *2 servings.*

Double-deck Potatoes and Carrots

2 medium potatoes, cut in ¼" slices	1 tsp. salt
½ cup boiling water	1 tbsp. milk
2 medium carrots, cut in sticks	⅓ cup grated American cheese

Place potatoes in boiling water in heavy covered saucepan; place carrots on top of potatoes. Sprinkle with salt. Cover and cook over medium heat for about 5 min. Reduce heat; simmer 20 to 25 min. (You may have to add more water if saucepan is not tightly covered.) When potatoes and carrots are tender, drain and add milk; sprinkle with grated cheese. Replace cover; turn off heat and allow cheese to melt. *2 servings.*

Orange-Bermuda Onion Salad

Alternate slices of orange with rings of Bermuda onion. Top with Ruby Red Dressing (below).

Ruby Red Dressing

½ cup currant jelly	dash of salt
¼ cup vegetable oil	few drops of onion
2 tbsp. lemon juice	juice

Beat jelly with fork until smooth. Add remaining ingredients; beat again until smooth. *Makes ¾ cup.*

Vanilla Custard Pudding

2 tbsp. sugar	1 egg yolk, slightly beaten
1 tbsp. cornstarch	
⅛ tsp. salt	1½ tsp. butter
1 cup milk	½ tsp. vanilla

Mix sugar, cornstarch, and salt in saucepan. Gradually stir in milk. Place over medium heat, stirring constantly. Bring to boil; boil gently 1 min. Slowly pour at least half of hot mixture into egg yolk, stirring constantly. Pour into remaining hot mixture in saucepan; return to heat and boil gently 1 min. more. Remove from heat. Add butter and vanilla. Cool, stirring occasionally to keep skin from forming. Chill in refrigerator. Serve with cream. *2 servings.*

Chocolate Custard Pudding

Make Vanilla Custard Pudding (above)—except add 2 tbsp. more sugar with 1 sq. unsweetened chocolate (1 oz.), cut up, with the milk.

Wednesday

For Wednesday's dinner, perk up midweek appetites by featuring a fresh fruit or vegetable. Choose a menu from "Seasonal Favorites" and consult the marketing tips in the "Cook's Primer."

Autumn Soup
Crisp Vegetable Sticks
Sweet Cucumber Pickles
Cheese-topped English Muffins
Hot Gingerbread with Lemon Sauce

Autumn Soup

½ lb. ground beef	¼ tsp. pepper
½ cup chopped onions	½ bay leaf, crumbled
2 cups hot water	pinch of basil
¾ cup cut-up celery	3 whole fresh tomatoes,
¾ cup cut-up potatoes	stems removed
1 tsp. salt	

Brown ground beef slowly in a little hot fat in a heavy kettle. Add onions and cook 5 min. more. Add remaining ingredients except tomatoes and mix thoroughly, loosening the brown crustiness from bottom of kettle. Bring to boil; cover, then simmer 20 min. Add tomatoes and, if necessary, more water; simmer 10 min. longer. *2 generous servings.*

Crisp Vegetable Sticks

Cut chilled raw vegetables lengthwise into thin sticks. Carrots, cucumbers, turnips, or beets are good choices. A decorative touch may be added by stringing pitted green or ripe olives on the sticks.

Cheese-topped English Muffins

Split 2 English muffins crosswise with a knife or pull them apart with a fork. Spread cut sides with butter. Toast, buttered-side-up, under broiler. Top with a slice of Cheddar or process cheese. Return to broiler until cheese is melted.

Hot Gingerbread

Heat oven to 350° (mod.). Grease and flour an 8″ pie pan. Measure the contents of 1 pkg. (14.5 oz.) gingerbread mix; divide in half. Empty one half into small mixer bowl. Stir in ½ cup lukewarm water. Beat 2 min. medium speed on mixer (300 strokes by hand). Pour into prepared pan. Bake 20 to 25 min. Serve in wedges.

To reheat gingerbread, wrap in foil; heat in 375° oven for 20 min.

Lemon Sauce

¼ cup sugar	1½ tsp. lemon juice
1½ tsp. cornstarch	1½ tsp. grated lemon
½ cup water	rind
1½ tsp. butter	

Mix sugar and cornstarch. Gradually stir in water. Cook over medium heat, stirring constantly until mixture thickens and boils. Boil 1 min. Remove from heat. Stir in remaining ingredients. Keep hot until time to serve. Serve over gingerbread. *Makes ⅔ cup sauce.*

Creamy Lemon Sauce

Beat ½ cup soft butter and ½ pkg. (14.3-oz. size) lemon frosting mix until creamy. Whip ½ cup whipping cream; fold into frosting mixture. Heat, stirring constantly; boil until foamy. Serve immediately. *Makes 1 to 1½ cups.*

Thursday

By Thursday, if you're stretching the budget, take your cue from "Frankly Thrifty." You'll be serving a delicious meal and pinching pennies at the same time—a painless way to save!

Baked Beans with Canadian Bacon
Mixed Vegetable Salad
Dark Date Nut Bread
Baked Apples

Speedy Baked Beans

2 strips bacon, diced	½ tsp. prepared
1 small onion, minced	mustard
1 can (1 lb.) baked	2 tbsp. chili sauce
beans with pork	

Heat oven to 350° (mod.). Sauté bacon and onion until bacon is crisp and onion yellow. Stir in remaining ingredients. Pour into greased 1-qt. baking dish. Bake uncovered 45 min., until the beans are brown and bubbling. Serve hot. *2 generous servings.*

Baked Beans with Canadian Bacon

Serve Speedy Baked Beans (above) with slices of hot broiled or fried Canadian bacon.

Baked Beans with Ham

Add 1 cup cut-up baked ham to Speedy Baked Beans (above).

Mixed Vegetable Salad

1 cup torn chilled	Oil-and-Vinegar
salad greens	Dressing (p. 59)
1 cup chopped vege-	
tables (raw or	
chilled cooked)	

Toss greens and vegetables together with just enough dressing to coat greens. *2 servings.*

Note: Cut-up mixed vegetables are available in an 8-oz. can—just one cup.

Dark Date Nut Bread

½ cup boiling water	¾ cup plus 2 tbsp.
½ cup mixed light	all-purpose flour
and dark raisins	½ cup sugar
½ cup chopped dates	¼ tsp. salt
1½ tbsp. butter	1 egg
¾ tsp. soda	½ tsp. vanilla
	¼ cup chopped nuts

Heat oven to 350° (mod.). Pour boiling water over raisins, dates, butter, and soda; let stand. Measure flour by dipping method (p. 123) or by sifting. Mix flour, sugar, and salt well; add fruit mixture and remaining ingredients. Beat well; pour into greased and floured 1-lb. coffee can. Bake 60 to 70 min.

Leftover Dark Bread can be covered with transparent plastic wrap or aluminum foil and stored in refrigerator or freezer.

To save time, use canned brown bread. It's easy to heat in oven or over hot water.

Baked Apples

Choose baking apples such as Rome Beauty, Jonathan, Wealthy, or Greening.

Heat oven to 350° (mod.). Wash and then core apples. Either pare upper half of apples or pare one strip around center. Place in baking dish; fill center of each apple with 1 to 2 tbsp. granulated or brown sugar, 1 tsp. butter, and ⅛ tsp. cinnamon. Cover bottom of pan with water about ¼″ deep. Bake uncovered 45 to 60 min., or until tender when pierced with fork (time varies). Baste occasionally. Serve plain or with cream.

Baked Apples Vermont

Bake apples as directed above—except fill center of each apple with 1 tsp. butter and 1 tbsp. maple syrup.

Friday

Friday ushers in the weekend—for some, it's payday, a good time to splurge a little. Make a specialty for dinner—consider a menu from "Regional Favorites" to add variety and interest to the week.

Chef's Salad or Crab Louis
Hot Potato Chips (p. 21)
Beaten Raisin Bread
Fresh Fruit in Season
Mary's Sugar Cookies (p. 30)

Chef's Salad

½ head lettuce
¼ bunch romaine or endive
¼ cup chopped green onion
¼ cup sliced celery
¼ cup julienne strips of cold cooked meat (such as beef, ham, tongue, luncheon meat)
¼ cup julienne strips of cold cooked chicken or turkey
½ cup julienne strips of Swiss cheese
fillets of anchovy, if desired
¼ cup mayonnaise
2 tbsp. French Dressing (p. 25)
4 ripe olives
1 hard-cooked egg, sliced

Tear greens into bite-sized pieces. Toss greens with onion, celery, meat, chicken, cheese, and anchovies, reserving a few strips of meat, chicken, and cheese for garnish. Just before serving, toss with dressings. Garnish with reserved julienne strips, ripe olives, and hard-cooked egg. *2 servings.*

Crab Louis

2 cups salad greens, torn into bite-sized pieces
1 can (7½ oz.) or frozen pkg. (7 oz.) crabmeat chunks
2 tomatoes, quartered
2 hard-cooked eggs, quartered
ripe or green olives
Louis Dressing (right)

Arrange chilled salad greens in individual salad bowls. Top with chilled crabmeat, tomatoes, eggs, and olives. Pour Louis Dressing over salad. *2 servings.*

Louis Dressing

¼ cup plus 2 tbsp. chili sauce
½ tsp. freshly minced onion
⅛ tsp. Worcestershire sauce
¼ cup mayonnaise
¼ tsp. sugar
salt to taste

Mix ingredients. Refrigerate 30 min. before pouring over Crab Louis. *Makes ½ cup.*

Beaten Raisin Bread

1 pkg. active dry yeast
1¼ cups warm water (not hot—110 to 115°)
2 tbsp. sugar
4 cups buttermilk baking mix
⅔ cup raisins

In mixing bowl, dissolve yeast in warm water. Add sugar and half of baking mix. Beat 2 min. medium speed on mixer or 300 vigorous strokes by hand. Scrape sides and bottom of bowl frequently. Add remaining baking mix and raisins; blend well until smooth. Scrape sides and bottom of bowl. Cover with a cloth and let rise in warm place (85°) until double, about 30 min. (If kitchen is cool, place dough on a rack over a bowl of hot water and cover completely with a towel.) Stir down batter by beating about 25 strokes. Spread batter evenly in greased loaf pan, 8½ x 4½ x 2¾". Batter will be sticky. Smooth out top of loaf by flouring hands and patting into shape. Again, let rise in warm place (85°) until batter reaches ¼" from top of pan, 30 to 40 min.

Heat oven to 375° (quick mod.). Bake 45 to 50 min., or until well browned. To test loaf, tap top crust—it should sound hollow. Immediately remove from pan. Place on cooling rack. Brush top with melted butter or shortening. Cool before cutting.

Leftover Raisin Bread? Try it toasted for breakfast. It's a delightful treat!

Saturday

If you entertain on Saturday—and this may be traditional—plan a dinner party for four or a buffet supper for more. You'll find wonderful menus that make party-giving a pleasure in "When Company Comes."

*Party Bake Pork Chops
Italian Green Beans with Mushrooms
Peanut Crunch Slaw
Popovers (p. 85)
Portia's Pears*

Party Bake Pork Chops

4 lean pork chops, 1" thick	1 can (1 lb. 13 oz.) tomatoes
4 thin slices onion	½ to 1 tsp. salt
¼ cup uncooked rice (not instant)	pepper

Trim any excess fat from chops. Season chops well on both sides with salt and pepper. Brown on both sides in lightly greased hot skillet. Top each chop with a slice of onion, 1 tbsp. rice, and cover with whole tomatoes. Add any remaining tomatoes and juice to skillet. Season with salt. Cover tightly; simmer over low heat or bake in foil-covered baking dish, 11½ x 7½ x 1½", in 350° (mod.) oven 1½ hr., or until tender. *4 servings.*

Peanut Crunch Slaw

2 cups shredded cabbage	2 tbsp. chopped green pepper
½ cup finely cut celery	¼ cup chopped cucumber
¼ cup commercial sour cream	¼ cup salted peanuts, coarsely chopped
¼ cup mayonnaise	
½ tsp. salt	
2 tbsp. chopped green onion	

Toss cabbage and celery together. Chill. Mix sour cream, mayonnaise, salt, onion, green pepper, and cucumber; chill. Just before serving, toss chilled vegetables with dressing. Sprinkle chopped peanuts on top. *4 servings.*

Italian Green Beans with Mushrooms

Cook 1 pkg. (10 oz.) frozen Italian green beans according to pkg directions—except add 1 can (3 oz.) mushrooms the last few min. of cooking time. Drain. *4 servings.*

Portia's Pears

Use 2 small canned pear halves for each serving. Moisten cocoa (1 tbsp. for each pear) with some pear juice. Fill center cavity of 1 half. Place 2 halves together; fasten with toothpick. Chill. Serve in dessert dishes topped with Quick Custard Sauce (below).

Quick Custard Sauce

Prepare vanilla pudding and pie filling mix using 1½ times as much milk as recipe on pkg. calls for. Serve warm.

Leftover Sauce? Refrigerate and use for a simple dessert or over fruit.

"Party-Starter" Beverages

These are nice to serve chilled with an appetizer in the living room while guests are arriving and the hostess does last-minute duties in the kitchen.

Tomato Juice	Cranberry Juice
Vegetable Cocktail Juice	Cider
Clam Juice	Ginger Ale
Sauerkraut Juice	Catawba Grape Juice
Beef Bouillon on the Rocks	(sparkling white or red)

To make enough Popovers for four, simply double the recipe on p. 85.

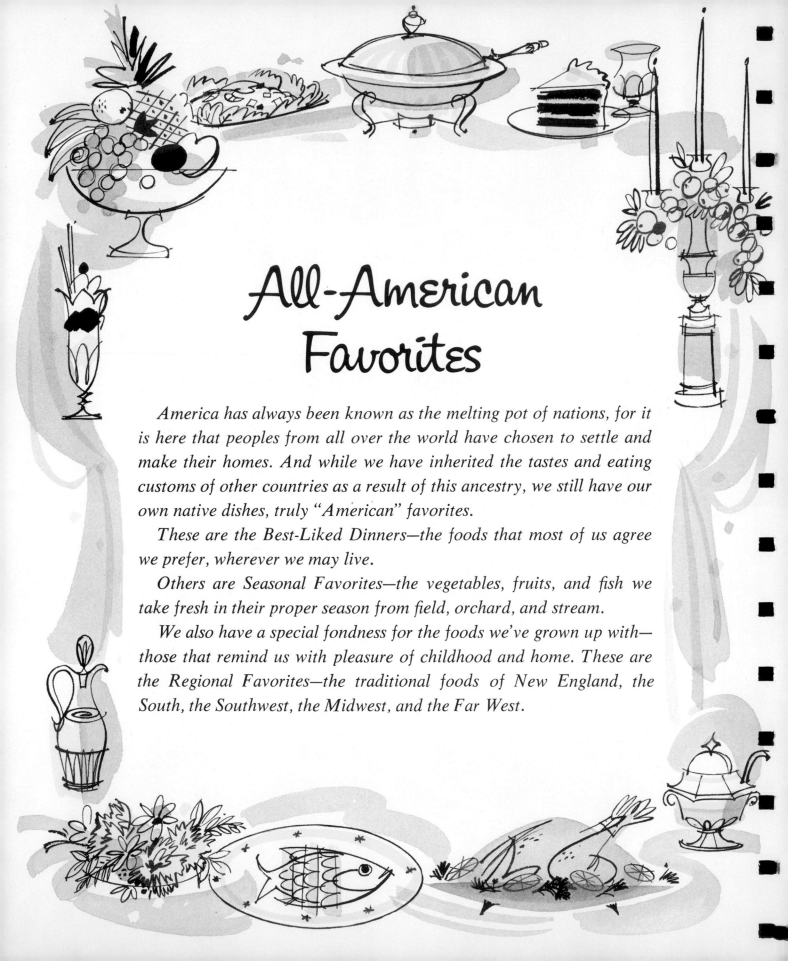

All-American Favorites

America has always been known as the melting pot of nations, for it is here that peoples from all over the world have chosen to settle and make their homes. And while we have inherited the tastes and eating customs of other countries as a result of this ancestry, we still have our own native dishes, truly "American" favorites.

These are the Best-Liked Dinners—the foods that most of us agree we prefer, wherever we may live.

Others are Seasonal Favorites—the vegetables, fruits, and fish we take fresh in their proper season from field, orchard, and stream.

We also have a special fondness for the foods we've grown up with— those that remind us with pleasure of childhood and home. These are the Regional Favorites—the traditional foods of New England, the South, the Southwest, the Midwest, and the Far West.

"...From Sea to Shining Sea"

Coast to coast, and according to the growing seasons of each region, America the beautiful abounds in richly varied native foods. And the pleasures of a whole new way of dining can be found in every section of this land. Following are some of these regional specialties whose very names whet the appetite, delight the taste, and linger happily in our memories.

THE FAR WEST

Abalone
Apple Dumplings
Avocado Salad
Bean Sprouts
Columbia Salmon
Eggs Foo Yung
Fresh Figs and Dates
Honeydew Melon
Jack Cheese
Kumquats
Mountain Trout
Orange Juice
Pheasant
Ripe Olives
Spanish Omelet
Tiny Pacific Shrimp
Venison Steak
Walnuts
Water Chestnuts

THE SOUTHWEST

Barbecued Beef
Chili con Carne
Frijoles
Grapefruit
Hot Chocolate
Lettuces
Melons
Prickly Pears
Sour Cream Pies
Summer Squash
Tortillas

THE SOUTH

Baked Ham
Baking Powder
  Biscuits
Black-eyed Peas
Deep-dish Peach Pie
Deviled Crab
Fritters
Frogs Legs
Hominy Grits
Oysters Rockefeller
Pecan Pralines
Shrimp Gumbo
Spoon Bread
Terrapin
Watermelon

THE MIDWEST

Bacon and Eggs
Cherry Pie Cobbler
Corn on the Cob
Green String Beans
Honey and Biscuits
Mashed Potatoes
Mushroom Gravy
Pork Chops
Pumpkin Pie
Roast Beef
Roast Turkey
Rutabagas
Smelts
Steak
Sweet Cider

NEW ENGLAND

Anadama Bread
Boston Baked Beans
  and Brown Bread
Boston Cream Pie
Broiled Lobster with
  Drawn Butter
Clam Chowder
Codfish Cakes
Cornmeal Pancakes
  and Real Maple
  Syrup
Cranberry Sauce
Gooseberry Tarts
Indian Pudding with
  Nutmeg Sauce
Succotash

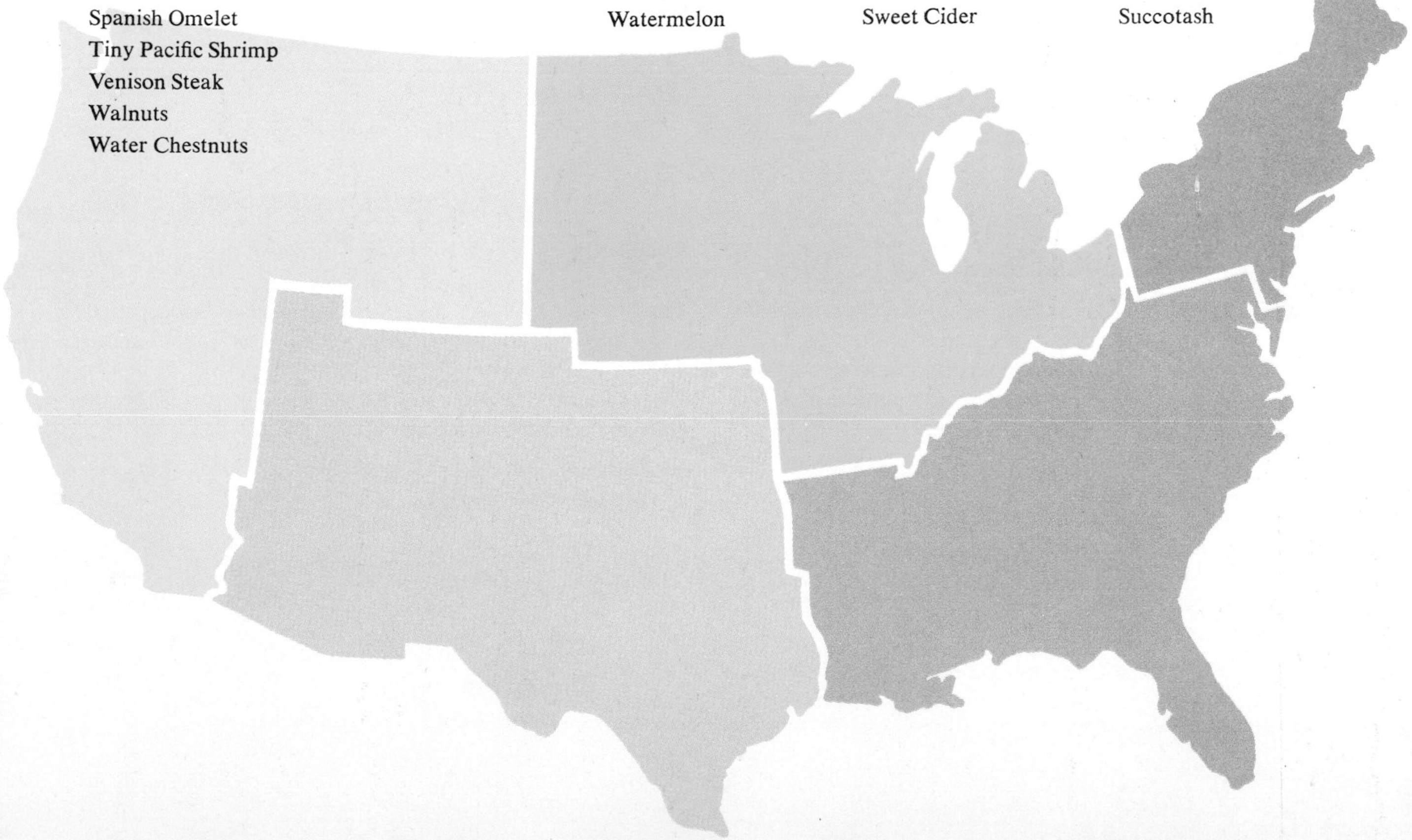

Best-Liked Dinners

East side, west side—and all around the country—a juicy roast beef, ice cream and brownies, hamburgers, French fries, and half a dozen other tried-and-true dishes are almost everybody's favorite typically American foods. These are the dishes that have stood the test of time and change.

Baked Ham
Scalloped Potatoes
Whole Carrots (p. 113)
Molded Lime-Pineapple Salad
Brown 'N Serve Rolls
Chocolate Custard Pudding (p. 9)

Schedule for Dinner on Time

Ahead of time:
Prepare pudding; refrigerate.
Prepare salad.

1½ hr. ahead:
Prepare potatoes; begin baking.

At time determined by canned ham:
Bake ham.

30 min. ahead:
Prepare carrots; start cooking.
Set table.
Arrange salad on plates; refrigerate.

20 min. ahead:
Remove ham from oven.

10 min. ahead:
Heat dinner rolls.
Whip cream for dessert.

Baked Ham

Place a small canned ham fat-side-up on rack in baking pan. Bake as directed on can. About 30 min. before ham is done, remove from oven. Pour off drippings and score ham with sharp knife, making diagonal cuts across entire top surface to form diamond shapes. Stud corners of diamonds with whole cloves. Mix ½ cup brown sugar with enough syrup from canned pineapple, peaches, or pears to moisten. Spread on ham. Return to oven to finish baking, basting occasionally with the fruit juice.

Allow ham to stand 20 min. after removing from oven. It will slice better.

Leftovers? Use leftover baked ham in sandwiches, Chef's Salad (p. 13), or Au Gratin Potatoes with Ham (p. 75). Also refer to the index.

Scalloped Potatoes

4 cups thinly sliced pared potatoes	1 tsp. salt
¼ cup minced onion	¼ tsp. pepper
3 tbsp. flour	¼ cup butter
	2½ cups hot milk

Heat oven to 350° (mod.). Arrange potatoes in four layers in 2-qt. casserole. Sprinkle the first 3 layers with 1 tbsp. onion, 1 tbsp. flour, ¼ tsp. salt, and dash of pepper. Sprinkle last layer with remaining onion, salt, and pepper; dot with butter. Pour *hot* milk over potatoes and bake covered 30 min. Bake uncovered 60 to 70 min. longer. *4 servings.*

Hurry-up Scalloped Potatoes

Heat oven to 400° (mod. hot). Measure potatoes and sauce mix from 1 pkg. (5.5 oz.) scalloped potatoes; divide in half. Empty potato slices into 1-qt. baking dish and sprinkle with sauce mix. Add half the amounts of butter, water, and milk called for on the pkg.; stir thoroughly. Bake uncovered 30 to 35 min. Serve immediately. *2 to 3 servings.*

Note: It is best to use remaining half pkg. of potatoes within 2 weeks.

Molded Lime-Pineapple Salad

Prepare 1 pkg. (3 oz.) lime-flavored gelatin as directed on pkg. Chill until slightly thickened. Stir in 1 can (9 oz.) crushed pineapple, drained. Spoon mixture into 4 to 6 individual molds. (For 2 to 3 servings, use only ½ pkg. gelatin, ½ amount of water, and ½ amount of fruit.) Chill until firm. Serve on lettuce; top with mayonnaise.

Leftover Salad? Use as dessert the next day; top with whipped cream.

Roast Beef au Jus
Browned Potatoes
Tomatoes Vinaigrette (p. 73)
Hot Rolls
Ice Cream
with Raspberry-Currant Sauce
Brownies

Schedule for Dinner on Time

Ahead of time:
Mix dressing for Tomatoes Vinaigrette; prepare tomatoes and marinate.
Bake Brownies.
Make Raspberry-Currant Sauce.

At time determined by size of roast:
Put roast in oven.
Boil potatoes.

30 min. ahead:
Add potatoes to roast. Set table.

5 min. ahead:
Heat rolls.

Roast Beef

For best flavor and least shrinkage a beef roast should weigh at least 4 lb.

Choose: Standing Rib, Rolled Rib

Heat oven to 325° (slow mod.). Season meat with salt and pepper. Place fat-side-up on rack in open pan. Standing rib roast needs no rack. If you have a meat thermometer, insert through outside fat into thickest part of meat. Do not baste, cover, or add water.

When meat is roasted as desired (see chart below), serve immediately on hot platter with Browned Potatoes (right) and parsley garnish on either side. Serve brown meat juices in a separate bowl.

Leftover Beef? Refer to the index for recipes that call for cooked beef.

	Min. per Lb.	Meat Temp.
Rare:	26 to 32	140°
Medium:	34 to 38	160°
Well Done:	40 to 44	170°

For rolled roasts, allow maximum time as shown in chart above.

Browned Potatoes

Pare 2 or 3 medium potatoes. Cook in 2″ boiling salted water about 20 min., until almost done. Drain. Add to roast last 30 min.; turn potatoes to brown evenly. *2 servings.*

Raspberry-Currant Sauce

1 pkg. (10 oz.) frozen
  raspberries, thawed
½ cup currant jelly

1 tbsp. cold water
½ tbsp. cornstarch

Mix raspberries and jelly; bring to boil. Make paste of water and cornstarch; stir into boiling mixture Boil 1 min., stirring constantly. Cool and strain. Store covered in refrigerator. Serve over vanilla ice cream. *Makes 1⅓ cups.*

Brownies

2 sq. unsweetened
  chocolate (2 oz.)
⅓ cup shortening
1 cup sugar
2 eggs

¾ cup all-purpose
  flour
½ tsp. baking powder
½ tsp. salt
½ cup broken nuts

Heat oven to 350° (mod.). Generously grease a square pan, 8x8x2″. Melt chocolate and shortening together over low heat. Beat in sugar and eggs. Measure flour by dipping method (p. 123) or by sifting. Blend flour, baking powder, and salt; stir into chocolate mixture. Mix in nuts. Spread in pan. Bake 30 to 35 min., until top has dull crust. A slight imprint will remain when touched lightly with finger. Cool slightly. Cut in 2″ squares. *Makes 16 brownies.*

To save time, make Brownies with brownie mix. Easy directions on pkg.

Broiled Hamburgers
Creamy Cole Slaw   Hot Potato Chips
Chilled Apricots
Date Bar Drop Cookies (p. 93)

Schedule for Dinner on Time

Ahead of time:
　Chill apricots.
　Bake cookies.
　Make salad dressing.

30 min. ahead:
　Prepare cabbage; refrigerate.
　Set table.
　Shape hamburger patties.

10 min. ahead:
　Begin broiling hamburgers.

5 min. ahead:
　Put buns under broiler.
　Toss cabbage with dressing.
　Heat potato chips.

Broiled Hamburgers

½ lb. ground beef	¼ cup water or milk
½ tsp. salt	Worcestershire sauce,
⅛ tsp. pepper	horseradish, or
1 tbsp. chopped onion	mustard to taste

Toss all ingredients together lightly. Shape gently into 2 balls and flatten to ¾″ thickness. Brush lightly with melted butter or vegetable oil. Broil on metal pie pan 3″ from heat, turning once. Broil 4 to 6 min. on each side, depending on how rare you like your meat. Serve immediately on buttered toasted split buns. If desired, garnish with slices of tomato and Bermuda onion, or chili sauce and onion. *2 servings.*

Burgers with a Bonus

Make Hamburgers (above)—except after they have broiled 5 min., pour a little barbecue sauce (bottled or made from your favorite recipe) over them. Broil 5 to 10 min., basting often.

Southern Burgers

A tangy hamburger variation.

½ lb. ground beef	1½ tbsp. prepared
1 small onion, diced	mustard
1½ tbsp. catsup	½ can chicken gumbo
	soup (10½-oz.
	can)

Brown beef and onion in a little hot fat in skillet. Stir in catsup, mustard, and soup. Simmer until mixture has thickened a little, about 15 min. Spoon over toasted split buns or English muffin halves. *2 servings.*

Note: Dilute and heat leftover soup for lunch another day.

Creamy Cole Slaw

Just before serving dinner, toss 1½ cups finely chopped or shredded cabbage with ⅓ cup Creamy Boiled Dressing (below).
　To shred cabbage, use sharp kitchen knife. Cut ¼ of a medium head, saving remainder for later use. Cut this quarter into 2 halves. Place cabbage on cutting board with flat side down. Shred finely, never lifting point of knife from board. Or use a shredder, setting blade for fine or coarse shredding. *2 servings.*

Waldorf-style Slaw

Make Creamy Cole Slaw (above)—except substitute cut-up red apple, celery, and nuts for part of cabbage.

Creamy Boiled Dressing

¼ cup sweet or	1½ tsp. sugar
commercial sour	¼ tsp. dry mustard
cream	dash of freshly ground
1 egg yolk	pepper
1 tbsp. vinegar	pinch of dill seed, if
¼ tsp. salt	desired

Mix ingredients in top of double boiler. Cook over hot water until mixture begins to thicken, stirring constantly. Cool. Store in covered jar in refrigerator. *Makes ⅓ cup.*

　　HOW TO HEAT POTATO CHIPS
　Spread on baking sheet. Slide into hot oven a few minutes (watch carefully—they burn).

Chilled Apricots

One can (8 oz.) apricots should be just right for two. Be sure they are well chilled.

✱✱✱✱✱✱✱✱✱✱✱✱✱✱✱✱✱✱
✱   ✱
✱   *Roast Pork*   ✱
✱   *Cinnamon Apple Rings*   ✱
✱   *Browned Potatoes (p. 20)*   ✱
✱   *Pan Gravy (p. 121)*   ✱
✱   *Baked Squash   Batter Buns*   ✱
✱   *Perfection Salad (p. 32)*   ✱
✱   *Lemon Pudding Cake*   ✱
✱   ✱
✱✱✱✱✱✱✱✱✱✱✱✱✱✱✱✱✱✱

Schedule for Dinner on Time

Ahead of time:
   Prepare Perfection Salad; refrigerate.
   Make Lemon Pudding Cake.
   Make Batter Buns.

At time determined by size of roast:
   Put roast in oven.

1 hr. ahead:
   Bake squash.
   Boil potatoes.

30 min. ahead:
   Add potatoes to roast.
   Turn squash.
   Set table.

10 min. ahead:
   Remove roast from oven; keep warm.
   Make gravy.
   Reheat buns.

Roast Pork

Allow ⅓ to ½ lb. with bone or ¼ to ⅓ lb. boneless for each serving.

Heat oven to 350° (mod.). Season meat with salt and pepper. Place fat-side-up in open pan. If you're using a meat thermometer, insert it through outside fat in thickest part of meat. Roast according to chart below. (*Always* roast pork until it is *well done*—cooked lean pork should be grayish-white without a tinge of pink.)

When roast is done, remove to hot platter and keep warm (cover roast with aluminum foil) while making Pan Gravy.

	Min. per Lb.	Meat Temp.
Loin	35 to 40	185°
Leg	25 to 40	185°
Shoulder	35 to 40	185°

For rolled roasts, add 10 min. per lb.

Leftover Pork? See the entry for pork in the index.

Baked Squash

Wash an acorn squash and cut lengthwise in half or quarters. Remove seeds. Brush with butter; season with salt and pepper. Heat oven to 350° (mod.). Bake squash halves cut-side-down in shallow pan 30 min. Turn squash; bake until tender, about 30 min. more. Brush again with butter; season with salt and pepper. *2 servings.*

Batter Buns

After roast is out, raise oven temperature and reheat buns.

⅔ cup warm water (not hot—110 to 115°)	½ tsp. salt
	¼ cup soft shortening
1 pkg. active dry yeast	1 egg
2 tbsp. sugar	1⅔ cups all-purpose flour

Measure water into mixer bowl. Add yeast, stirring to dissolve. Measure flour by dipping method (p. 123) or by sifting. Add sugar, salt, shortening, egg, and 1 cup of the flour. Combine with mixer on low speed, guiding batter into beaters with rubber scraper. Add the remaining flour. Beat with scraper until smooth. Spoon into greased muffin cups, filling each a scant ½ full.

Let rise in warm place (85°) until batter reaches top of muffin cups, 30 to 40 min.

Heat oven to 375° (quick mod.). Bake 18 to 20 min., until golden brown. Serve warm. *Makes about 12 buns.*

To reheat buns and rolls, wrap in aluminum foil or place in paper bag and sprinkle bag with water. Heat in 400° (mod. hot) oven for 10 min.

Lemon Pudding Cake

2 tbsp. flour	1 egg yolk, well beaten
½ cup sugar	
⅛ tsp. salt	½ cup milk
1½ tsp. grated lemon rind	1 egg white, stiffly beaten
2 tbsp. lemon juice	

Heat oven to 350° (mod.). Mix flour, sugar, and salt. Stir in lemon rind, lemon juice, egg yolk, and milk. Fold in stiffly beaten egg white. Pour into two 3″ custard cups. Set in pan of hot water 1″ deep. Bake 50 min. Serve warm or cold, with or without whipped cream. *2 servings.*

To save time, use lemon pudding cake mix—tangy, easy.

Regional Favorites

Wherever our pioneer forefathers settled and put down roots, they took the abundant native foods of the region and made them into dishes that reflected the tastes of the homelands they left behind. And so America's regional food specialties and dining customs developed—a heritage we enjoy today in New England's seafood plates and boiled dinners, the gracious hospitality of the South, the hearty fare of the Midwest, the spicy flavorings of the Southwest, and the casual, colorful meals of the Far West.

****

Boiled Dinner
Horseradish Sauce (p. 122)
Anadama Bread
Vanilla Custard Pudding (p. 9)

****

Boiled Dinner

2-lb. corned brisket of beef	1 turnip, cubed (if desired)
2 small onions	½ green cabbage, cut in wedges
4 whole carrots	Horseradish Sauce (p. 122)
2 potatoes, halved or quartered	

Place beef in heavy kettle. Cover with hot water. Cover tightly and simmer 2½ to 3 hr., until tender. Remove meat and keep warm. Skim off excess fat and add onions, carrots, potatoes, and turnip. Cover and cook 15 min. Add cabbage and cook another 10 min. Serve with Horseradish Sauce. *4 servings.*

Leftover Corned Beef? Use in tasty Red Flannel Hash (p. 67) made with corned beef, potatoes, and beets. Or make sandwiches of thinly sliced corned beef.

Anadama Bread

¾ cup boiling water	¼ cup warm water (not hot—110 to 115°)
½ cup yellow corn meal	
3 tbsp. shortening	2¾ cups all-purpose flour
¼ cup molasses	
2 tsp. salt	1 egg
1 pkg. active dry yeast	

In large mixing bowl, stir boiling water, corn meal, shortening, molasses, and salt. Cool to lukewarm. Dissolve yeast in warm water. Measure flour by dipping method (p. 123) or by sifting. Add yeast, egg, and half the flour to lukewarm mixture. Beat 2 min. medium speed on mixer or 300 vigorous strokes by hand. Scrape sides and bottom of bowl frequently. Add rest of flour and mix with spoon until thoroughly blended into dough.

Spread batter evenly in greased loaf pan, 8½ x 4½ x 2¾" or 9x5x3". Batter will be sticky. Smooth out top of loaf by flouring hand and patting into shape.

Let rise in warm place (85°) until batter reaches top of 8½" pan or 1" from top of 9" pan (about 1½ hr.). Sprinkle top with a little corn meal and salt.

Heat oven to 375° (quick mod.). Bake 50 to 55 min. To test loaf, tap the top crust; it should sound hollow. Crust will be dark brown. Immediately remove bread from pan. Place on cooling rack or across edges of bread pan. Brush top with melted butter or shortening. Do not place in direct draft. Cool before cutting.

Note: For individual loaves, spread batter evenly in 6 miniature greased loaf pans, 4¾ x 2⅝ x 1½". Proceed as directed above, letting rise until batter just reaches tops of pans. Bake 30 to 35 min.

✳✳✳✳✳✳✳✳✳✳✳✳✳✳✳✳✳
Pork Chops Supreme
Baked Potatoes   Creamed Asparagus
Lettuce with Roquefort Dressing
Fruited Gelatin
Snickerdoodles
✳✳✳✳✳✳✳✳✳✳✳✳✳✳✳✳✳

Pork Chops Supreme

Heat oven to 350° (mod.). Trim excess fat from 2 lean pork chops (1″ thick). Place chops in baking pan or dish. Salt well. Top each chop with a lemon slice and a thin onion slice; sprinkle generously with brown sugar. Pour 1 tbsp. catsup over each chop. Cover and bake 1 hr. Uncover and bake 30 min. longer, basting occasionally. *2 servings.*

Braised Pork Chops

Trim excess fat from 2 lean pork chops and use to lightly grease hot heavy skillet. Brown chops on both sides, allowing about 5 min. for each side. Add ¼ cup water; cover tightly. Cook slowly on top of range or bake in 350° (mod.) oven until tender and well done (see below). Season with salt and pepper. Serve immediately. *2 servings.*

	Thickness	Time
Rib or loin chops	1″	30 to 35 min.
Rib or loin chops	½″	20 min.
Shoulder chops	½″	20 min.

Baked Potatoes

Prick potato skin with fork. Bake in 375° (quick mod.) oven 1 hr. or in 350° (mod.) oven 1½ hr. For oven meals, temperature and time for potatoes may be adjusted.

Creamed Asparagus

1 lb. fresh asparagus	¼ tsp. salt
½ cup Medium White Sauce (p. 122)	dash of pepper

Wash asparagus; remove scales and break off stalks. Break stalks into 1″ lengths. Cook, covered, in 1″ boiling salted water 10 to 15 min. Meanwhile, prepare White Sauce. Add seasonings and drained cooked asparagus to the sauce. Stir gently. *2 servings.*

Roquefort Dressing

Mash ¼ cup Roquefort or Bleu cheese with ⅛ tsp. Worcestershire sauce. Blend in ½ cup French Dressing (below).

French Dressing, American Style

½ cup olive oil, vegetable oil, or combination	2 tbsp. lemon juice
	½ tsp. salt
	¼ tsp. each dry mustard and paprika
2 tbsp. vinegar	

Beat all ingredients together with rotary beater or shake well in tightly covered jar. Keep in covered jar in refrigerator. If dressing is made ahead of time, it may separate. If so, shake before using. *Makes about ½ cup.*

Fruited Gelatin

Prepare 1 pkg. (3 oz.) fruit-flavored gelatin according to pkg. directions. (For 2 to 3 servings, use only ½ pkg.) Add 1 to 2 cups drained cut-up fruit (fresh, canned, or thawed frozen). Pour into 5 to 6 individual molds. Chill until set. Serve with cream, whipped cream, or a soft custard.

Snickerdoodles

1 cup shortening (part butter)	2 tsp. cream of tartar
1½ cups sugar	1 tsp. soda
2 eggs	¼ tsp. salt
2¾ cups all-purpose flour	2 tbsp. sugar
	2 tsp. cinnamon

Heat oven to 400° (mod. hot). Mix shortening, sugar, and eggs thoroughly. Measure flour by dipping method (p. 123) or by sifting. Stir together flour, cream of tartar, soda, and salt; blend in. Form in 1″ balls. Roll in mixture of the 2 tbsp. sugar and cinnamon. Place about 2″ apart on ungreased baking sheet. Bake 8 to 10 min. *Makes about 6 doz. cookies.*

****

French Onion Soup
Shrimp Creole
on Fluffy White Rice
Green Salad (p. 59)   French Bread
Southern Ambrosia
Praline Squares

****

French Onion Soup

Prepare onion soup using canned soup. To serve: place a slice of toasted French bread in each soup bowl and pour hot soup over it. Sprinkle with Parmesan cheese. *2 servings.*

Shrimp Creole

¾ cup chopped onion (1 medium onion)
1 clove garlic, pressed or minced
1 medium green pepper, finely chopped
½ cup finely chopped celery
2 tbsp. butter
1 can (8 oz.) tomato sauce

½ cup water
1 bay leaf, crushed
1 tsp. minced fresh parsley
½ tsp. salt
scant ⅛ tsp. cayenne pepper
1 pkg. (7 oz.) frozen shrimp, thawed
Fluffy White Rice (below)

In medium skillet, sauté onion, garlic, green pepper, and celery in butter about 5 min., or until tender. Remove from heat; stir in tomato sauce, water, bay leaf, parsley, salt, and pepper. Simmer 10 min. Add additional water, if needed. Add thawed shrimp. Bring mixture to a boil; cook covered over medium heat 5 min. Serve Shrimp Creole over Fluffy White Rice. *2 generous servings.*

Fluffy White Rice

Drop ⅔ cup washed rice gradually into 1½ qt. boiling salted water (keep it boiling). Boil rapidly (lift to prevent sticking) until tender, 15 to 20 min. Kernels should feel soft. Drain; run boiling water through to separate kernels. Cover with cloth; set over boiling water until fluffy. Or transfer rice to ovenproof bowl, cover with aluminum foil, and keep warm in oven until fluffy and ready to serve. *2 servings.*

To save time, use instant rice.

Southern Ambrosia

Sprinkle orange slices with confectioners' sugar. Chill. Just before serving, top with flaked coconut.

Praline Squares

¼ cup shortening
1 cup light brown sugar (packed)
1 egg
¾ cup all-purpose flour

1 tsp. baking powder
½ tsp. salt
½ tsp. vanilla
½ cup chopped pecans

Heat oven to 350° (mod.). Grease and flour a square pan, 8x8x2″. Melt shortening over low heat. Remove from heat and blend in brown sugar; cool. Stir in egg. Measure flour by dipping method (p. 123) or by sifting. Mix flour, baking powder, and salt; stir in. Stir in vanilla and pecans. Spread in prepared pan. Bake 25 min., until a light touch with finger leaves slight imprint. Don't overbake! Cut into bars while warm. *Makes eighteen 2x1″ bars.*

Note: They'll keep soft and moist if stored in a tightly covered jar.

✳✳✳✳✳✳✳✳✳✳✳✳✳✳✳✳✳✳

Guacamole
Beef with Raisin Sauce
Green Beans with Mushrooms
Cauliflower Salad
Spicy Pumpkin Custard

✳✳✳✳✳✳✳✳✳✳✳✳✳✳✳✳✳✳

Guacamole

Combine 1 avocado, pitted; 1 small onion, minced; 1½ tsp. vinegar; salt and pepper to taste; and chopped green chili pepper to taste. Beat until smooth on medium mixer speed. Finely chop ½ peeled ripe tomato; fold into mixture. Serve Guacamole as a dip with corn chips.

Beef with Raisin Sauce

1 lb. round steak, 2″ thick	2 to 3 tbsp. water
2 cloves garlic, thinly sliced	1 tbsp. butter
1 tbsp. vegetable oil	⅓ cup raisins
½ tsp. salt	2 small tomatoes, skinned, chopped, and well drained
pinch of marjoram	pickled chilies

Make small, deep incisions in the meat, using a sharp knife; stuff with slices of garlic. Brown meat in oil in heavy skillet. Add salt, marjoram, and water. Cover tightly; simmer 1 hr., or until tender. If liquid cooks away, more may be added to prevent scorching. Meanwhile, melt butter in small skillet. Add raisins; sauté 10 min. Add tomatoes and heat through. Place steak on heated platter. Add raisin sauce to drippings in meat skillet; blend together. Pour over steak; garnish with chilies. *2 servings.*

Green Beans with Mushrooms

1 tbsp. minced onion	1 tsp. minced parsley
1 tbsp. vegetable oil	1 can (3 oz.) mushroom stems and pieces, drained
1 can (8 oz.) green beans, drained	salt and pepper
1 tbsp. cut-up pimiento	

Sauté onion in oil until transparent. Add beans, pimiento, parsley, and mushrooms. Season with salt and pepper. Fry together lightly to heat through. Turn into serving bowl. *2 servings.*

Cauliflower Salad

½ medium cauliflower, cooked	¼ tsp. oregano
1 green onion, finely chopped	¼ tsp. salt
1 tbsp. olive or vegetable oil	dash of pepper
1½ tsp. wine vinegar	grated Parmesan cheese
	parsley

Separate cauliflower into flowerettes. Add onion. Shake oil, vinegar, oregano, salt, and pepper to blend well. Pour over vegetables; toss lightly to coat well. Marinate 2 to 3 hr. Drain off excess dressing. Serve in salad bowl, sprinkled with cheese and garnished with sprigs of parsley. *2 servings.*

Spicy Pumpkin Custard

½ cup mashed cooked or canned pumpkin	2½ tbsp. granulated sugar
¼ tsp. salt	1½ tsp. butter
⅓ cup evaporated milk	¼ tsp. cinnamon
1 egg yolk	pinch each of ginger, nutmeg, and cloves

Heat oven to 350° (mod.). Blend all ingredients together with rotary beater. Pour into 2 custard cups. Place in pan of water 1″ deep. Bake 45 min., or until silver knife inserted 1″ from edge of custard cup comes out clean. Cool at least 20 min. Invert on dessert plates. *2 servings.*

✳✳✳✳✳✳✳✳✳✳✳✳✳✳✳✳✳✳✳

California Club Fruit Plate
(Crabmeat Salad in Avocado Halves)
Bread-and-Butter Sandwiches
Chocolate Cream Pie

✳✳✳✳✳✳✳✳✳✳✳✳✳✳✳✳✳✳✳

California Club Fruit Plate

For a beautiful arrangement, center each dinner plate with an avocado half (leave peel on) on lettuce. Fill with Crabmeat Salad (right).

At back of plate, on watercress, place mound of melon balls and seedless green grapes between finger sandwiches of lightly buttered dark and light bread or crusty French rolls. If desired, drip a little Sweet French Dressing (below) over the fruit.

At front of plate, arrange half-circle of orange slices topped with Walnut-Cheese Bonbons (right).

Sweet French Dressing

To ½ cup French Dressing (p. 25) add 1 tbsp. confectioners' sugar or honey.

Crabmeat Salad

½ cup flaked cooked crabmeat	½ cup diced celery
½ tsp. lemon juice	½ cup lettuce hearts in small pieces
½ tsp. finely minced onion	1 tbsp. mayonnaise
salt and paprika to taste	2 avocado halves

Mix all ingredients except mayonnaise and avocado. Chill thoroughly. Just before serving, drain and toss together with mayonnaise to moisten. Serve on avocado half. *2 servings.*

Walnut-Cheese Bonbons

Soften cream cheese with a little cream. Shape into balls, using 1 level tsp. for each. Place between walnut halves. You may make these ahead of time and refrigerate.

Chocolate Cream Pie

Prepare Baked 8″ Pie Shell (p. 127). Fill with chocolate cream filling, made as directed on pkg. of chocolate pudding and pie filling mix. Chill thoroughly (2 hr.) and top with sweetened whipped cream.

Seasonal Favorites

The 20th-century magic of freezing and canning brings us most foods in abundance the whole year through. Yet each season, in turn, offers foods at their natural best—fresh from field, waters, gardens, and orchards.
Whether we catch a fish and harvest fruits and vegetables with our own hands or whether we buy them at the market, we relish each at its peak of fresh perfection, adding new zest to eating at every change of season.

Roast Lamb
Pear Halves with Mint Jelly
Parsleyed Potatoes
Harvard Beets
Herb Bread (p. 124)
Rhubarb Sauce
Mary's Sugar Cookies

Roast Lamb

Choose a 2- to 2½-lb. sirloin roast. Heat oven to 325° (slow mod.). Season meat with salt and pepper. Place fat-side-up on rack in open pan. If you have a meat thermometer, insert it through outside fat in thickest part of meat. Roast 30 to 35 min. per lb., or until meat thermometer registers 175° (medium) or 182° (well done). Do not baste, do not cover, do not add water.

Serve on platter surrounded by potatoes and 2 or 3 canned pear halves filled with mint jelly. *4 to 6 servings.*

Leftover Lamb? See the entry for lamb in the index. You will find other uses for lamb there.

Parsleyed Potatoes

| 1 lb. new potatoes (4 medium) | 2 tbsp. butter |
| | 2 tbsp. minced parsley |

Wash potatoes thoroughly. Cook, covered, in boiling salted water 30 to 40 min., until tender. Pare. Melt butter in skillet, remove from heat, mix in parsley. Toss potatoes with mixture until coated. Serve at once. *2 servings.*

Harvard Beets

1½ tsp. cornstarch	1½ tsp. vinegar
2 tsp. sugar	1 can (8 oz.) diced beets, drained (1 cup)
¼ tsp. salt	
dash of pepper	
⅓ cup liquid (beet juice plus water to make ⅓ cup)	

Mix cornstarch, sugar, salt, and pepper. Combine beet liquid and vinegar; slowly blend into cornstarch mixture. Place over medium heat and bring to boil; boil 1 min. Add beets and heat through. *2 servings.*

Rhubarb Sauce

Wash and cut into 1″ pieces enough rhubarb to make 2 cups. Mix with ½ cup sugar and ¼ cup water in saucepan. Cook 10 to 15 min., until tender. Serve warm. *2 servings.*

Mary's Sugar Cookies

1½ cups sifted confectioners' sugar	½ tsp. almond flavoring
1 cup butter	2½ cups all-purpose flour
1 egg	1 tsp. soda
1 tsp. vanilla	1 tsp. cream of tartar

Mix sugar and butter. Mix in egg and flavorings. Measure flour by dipping method (p. 123) or by sifting. Blend dry ingredients; stir in. Refrigerate 2 to 3 hr.

Heat oven to 375° (quick mod.). Divide dough in half and roll out on lightly floured pastry cloth to 3/16″ thickness. Cut with floured cooky cutter. Sprinkle with sugar. Place on lightly greased baking sheet. Bake 7 to 8 min., or until delicately golden. *Makes 5 doz. 2 to 2½″ cookies.*

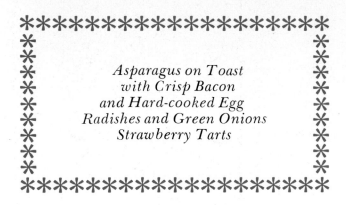

*Asparagus on Toast
with Crisp Bacon
and Hard-cooked Egg
Radishes and Green Onions
Strawberry Tarts*

Asparagus on Toast

1 lb. fresh asparagus	¼ cup melted butter or 1 cup Medium White Sauce (p. 122)
2 slices hot toast	
½ tsp. salt	
⅛ tsp. pepper	4 to 6 slices crisp bacon
	1 egg, hard-cooked

Break off asparagus stalks as far down as they snap easily. Remove scales along stems and wash well. Leave whole. Tie whole stalks in bunches with string and stand upright in narrow deep pan or coffeepot. Cook, covered, in 1″ boiling salted water 10 to 20 min., until tender crisp. Catch string with fork when lifting asparagus out of pan to keep stalks whole.

Arrange asparagus on slices of hot toast. Season with salt and pepper. Pour melted butter or hot White Sauce over the top. Garnish with crisp bacon strips and quartered hard-cooked egg. *2 servings.*

Asparagus on Ham Toast

Cook whole stalks of fresh asparagus (above), planning 5 to 6 stalks per serving. Make Cheese Sauce (p. 122). If time is short, make Cheese Sauce according to directions on can of cheese soup or heat canned or frozen Welsh Rarebit. Spread toast with deviled ham or top toast with slices of boiled ham. Arrange asparagus on ham toast and pour hot Cheese Sauce over toast. *2 servings.*

Strawberry Tarts

1 cup fresh strawberries	2 tbsp. brown sugar
½ cup commercial sour cream or	Short Pie Tart Shells (right)
½ cup whipped cream	

Mix berries with cream and brown sugar. Fill two tart shells. *2 servings.*

Short Pie Tart Shells

1 cup buttermilk baking mix	¼ cup soft butter
	3 tbsp. boiling water

Heat oven to 450° (hot). Blend baking mix and butter in bowl. Add boiling water and stir vigorously with fork until dough forms a ball and cleans the bowl. Dough will be puffy and soft. Divide into 6 parts. Pat out each piece on a 5″ circle of heavy-duty aluminum foil (use lid of coffee can to measure foil). Make tart shells by folding up an inch of foil and pinching in four corners. Place tarts on baking sheet. Bake 7 to 9 min., until lightly browned. Cool. Remove foil carefully. *Makes 6 tart shells.*

Leftover Tart Shells? Wrap loosely to store. Another day fill shells with ice cream and sundae sauce or with another fruit topped with whipped cream.

****

Baked or Pan-fried Fish
Green Beans and Corn
Cottage-fried Potatoes
Perfection Salad
Bread and Butter
Fresh Cherry Parfait

****

Baked or Pan-fried Fish

For two servings, choose a 1½- to 2-lb. pan fish (such as trout or sunfish) or ¾-lb. dressed fish or fillets. Sprinkle with salt and pepper. Dip in flour or buttermilk baking mix.

Baked: Heat oven to 500° (very hot). Place fish in lightly greased baking pan. Drizzle with 1 tbsp. melted butter. Bake 10 min. or until done. Serve immediately, garnished with lemon wedges.

Pan-fried: Pan-fry in 2 tbsp. hot fat (butter gives a delicious flavor) in heavy skillet 5 min., until golden brown on one side; turn and pan-fry 5 min. more, just until golden brown on other side. Serve immediately, garnished with lemon wedges.

Fish 'n Chips: Hot crisp potato chips are a wonderful accompaniment to tender fish fillets.

Green Beans and Corn

Wash and snap ends off ¼ lb. green beans. Cut French-style into lengthwise strips. Cook, uncovered, in ½″ boiling salted water for 5 min. Cover and finish cooking, about 5 min.

Cut corn from 2 cobs with a sharp knife. Cook in ½″ boiling unsalted water for 5 to 8 min. Lightly toss cooked beans, corn, butter, salt, and pepper. *2 servings.*

Cottage-fried Potatoes

Slice 3 to 4 boiled potatoes. Heap slices lightly into skillet with generous amount of heated butter or bacon drippings. Sprinkle with salt and pepper. Brown slowly, turning as sections brown. Cook 15 to 20 min., until crisp. *2 servings.*

Perfection Salad

½ pkg. lemon-flavored gelatin (3-oz. pkg.)	1 tbsp. finely chopped pimiento
1 tbsp. lemon juice	3 sweet pickles, chopped
½ cup finely shredded cabbage	½ tsp. salt
½ cup finely diced celery	

Prepare ½ pkg. of gelatin according to pkg. directions, reducing amount of liquid to half also. Stir in lemon juice. Chill until slightly thickened. Add remaining ingredients. Spoon into 2 individual molds. Chill until firm. Serve on lettuce; top with mayonnaise. *2 servings.*

Fresh Cherry Parfait

Layer fresh Bing cherry halves with vanilla ice cream in parfait glasses, allowing about ¼ cup fruit per serving. If desired, parfaits may be frozen 15 to 30 min. (If frozen longer than 1 hr., fruit will be icy and difficult to eat.)

****

Stuffed Green Peppers
Baked Potatoes (p. 25)
Carrot-Raisin Salad
Bread Sticks
Peach Bliss

****

Stuffed Green Peppers

3 large green peppers	½ cup coarse dry
1 cup boiling salted	bread or cracker
water (1½ tsp. salt)	crumbs
½ lb. ground beef	1 tsp. salt
1 can (8 oz.) tomato	¼ tsp. pepper
sauce	1 tbsp. chopped onion

Heat oven to 350° (mod.). Cut a thin slice from the stem end of each pepper. Wash outside and inside. Remove all seeds and membranes. Cook peppers in boiling salted water 5 min. Drain. Mix rest of ingredients. Stuff peppers lightly with mixture. Stand upright in small baking dish. Bake covered 45 min.; uncover and bake 15 min. more. *2 to 3 servings.*

Carrot-Raisin Salad

Mix together 1 cup grated carrots and 2 tbsp. raisins. Add just enough mayonnaise to hold mixture together. Serve in scoops on lettuce leaves. *2 servings.*

Bread Sticks

Bake ahead of time; reheat just before serving.

Make Biscuit dough as directed on buttermilk baking mix pkg.—except use ½ the amounts of ingredients. Roll into 6x4″ rectangle. Cut into 12 strips. Melt ¼ cup butter; pour half of it into a 9″ square pan. Pour remaining butter over tops of sticks which have been arranged in pan. Bake in 450° (hot) oven 10 to 15 min., until golden brown. *Makes 12 sticks.*

Corn Meal Bread Sticks: Follow recipe for Bread Sticks (above)—except substitute ½ cup corn meal for ½ cup of the baking mix. Sprinkle corn meal over melted butter in pan; salt sticks lightly before baking.

Peach Bliss

1 can (8 oz.) peach	dash of cinnamon
slices, drained	¼ tsp. almond
(reserve ½ cup	extract
syrup)	slices of white or
1½ tsp. cornstarch	yellow cake
¾ tsp. lemon juice	

Mix reserved syrup, cornstarch, lemon juice, and cinnamon in saucepan. Stir and cook mixture until it boils 1 min. Add almond extract and peach slices; heat through. Serve over cake slices. *2 servings.*

****

Brittany Duck en Casserole
Fluffy White Rice (p. 26)
Glazed Carrots
Green Salad (p. 59)
Rye Bread
Vanilla Parfait

****

Brittany Duck en Casserole

5- to 6-lb. duck, quartered	1 clove garlic, minced
1/3 cup all-purpose flour	3 tbsp. chopped parsley
2 tbsp. shortening	1 tbsp. paprika
finely chopped giblets and cubed liver	1 bay leaf
1 onion, finely chopped	1 tsp. salt
	1/4 tsp. pepper
	1/4 tsp. thyme
	1 cup apple cider

Heat oven to 350° (mod.). Wash and dry meat; shake in paper bag containing flour. Melt shortening in large heavy skillet. Brown meat well, 10 to 15 min. on each side. Remove excess fat with a baster as it accumulates. Remove meat from skillet, drain on absorbent paper and arrange with raw giblets and liver in 13x9½x2″ baking dish or Dutch oven. Sprinkle remaining ingredients over meat, leaving cider until last. Cover; bake 1½ to 2 hr., or until meat is tender. Baste frequently while baking. Remove from baking dish and drain on absorbent paper before serving. Garnish with fresh parsley. *4 to 6 servings.*

Leftover Duck? Cut in bite-sized pieces and use in chef's salads, or cooked macaroni or rice salads.

Glazed Carrots

4 medium carrots	1 tbsp. butter
1/4 cup sugar	2 tsp. carrot liquid

Wash and scrape carrots. Slice lengthwise. Cook, covered, in small amount of boiling salted water 10 to 15 min., until tender. Drain and reserve 2 tsp. liquid. In skillet, heat sugar, butter, and carrot liquid until blended. Add carrots and heat 8 to 10 min., until glazed and lightly browned. *2 servings.*

Vanilla Parfait

1 egg, separated	1 tsp. vanilla
1/2 cup whipping cream	1/2 cup crushed peppermint candy
1½ tbsp. sugar	

Beat egg white until stiff. Whip cream until stiff. Beat egg yolk with sugar until fluffy. Fold all ingredients together. Pile into mold or refrigerator tray. Freeze until firm (4 or 5 hr. or overnight). Serve on chilled dessert plates or in chilled parfait glasses. Garnish with crushed peppermint. *2 servings.*

****
Liver and Bacon Patties
Glazed Sweet Potatoes
Broiled Tomato Halves
Fruit Compote
Ginger Creams
****

Liver and Bacon Patties

1 cup boiling water	dash of pepper
½ lb. beef liver	½ cup crushed
½ small onion	whole wheat
1 egg	flakes cereal
½ tsp. salt	4 slices bacon

Pour boiling water over liver in pan; simmer gently 5 min. Remove liver and cool slightly. Grind liver and onion together. Mix with remaining ingredients except bacon. Shape into 4 patties; wrap each with a slice of bacon. Broil 3 to 4 inches from broiling unit until bacon is crisp and brown, 3 to 5 min. on each side. *2 servings.*

Glazed Sweet Potatoes

Brush tops of cooked sweet potato halves or slices with butter; sprinkle with brown sugar. Broil until sugar is bubbly, about 10 min.

Broiled Tomato Halves

Cut tomatoes into halves; sprinkle with salt, pepper, and basil. Top with buttered bread crumbs and broil 3 to 5 min.

Fruit Compote

2 cups mixed dried fruit (12 oz. pkg.), such as currants, raisins, prunes, pears, apricots, peaches, apples	3 cups water (half grape juice may be used)
	1 tbsp. tapioca
	¼ tsp. salt
	½ to ⅔ cup sugar
	1 stick cinnamon

Mix ingredients in saucepan; cook covered until fruits are tender (about 30 to 40 min.). Serve either hot or cold. Garnish with mint leaves or strawberries. *4 servings.*

Leftovers? Also delicious when served as a breakfast fruit or a meat accompaniment.

Ginger Creams

Add ½ cup lukewarm water to 1 pkg. (14.5 oz.) gingerbread mix. Blend until smooth. Mix in 1 cup canned pumpkin. Chill. Heat oven to 375° (quick mod.). Drop dough by teaspoonfuls onto lightly greased baking sheet. Bake 10 to 12 min. Frost tops with Browned Butter Icing (below). *Makes about 4 doz. cookies.*

Browned Butter Icing

3 tbsp. butter	1½ tbsp. cream
1½ cups sifted confectioners' sugar	¾ tsp. vanilla

Brown butter in saucepan over medium heat until delicately brown. Blend with sugar. Stir in cream and vanilla until smooth.

```
*********************
*                   *
*  Swiss Steak or Flank Steak  *
*      Mashed Potatoes          *
*   Buttered Brussels Sprouts   *
* Apple and Grapefruit Salad (p.75) *
*      Hard-crusted Rolls       *
*         Pecan Tarts           *
*                   *
*********************
```

Swiss Steak or Flank Steak
Mashed Potatoes
Buttered Brussels Sprouts
Apple and Grapefruit Salad (p. 75)
Hard-crusted Rolls
Pecan Tarts

Swiss Steak or Flank Steak

Rub Seasoned Flour (p. 6) into 2″-thick round steak or scored flank steak (¾ to 1 lb.).

Brown 1 onion, sliced, in hot fat in heavy skillet. Remove onion and brown meat well on both sides. Top with onion. Add ½ cup water, tomato juice, or vegetable juice. Cover tightly; cook slowly 1½ to 2 hr., until tender. If necessary, add more liquid during cooking. *2 servings.*

Mashed Potatoes

3 medium potatoes (1 lb.)	2 tbsp. butter
about ¼ cup hot milk	1 tsp. salt
	dash of pepper

Wash potatoes, then pare. Cook, tightly covered, in about 1½″ boiling salted water (1 tsp. salt) in heavy 1½-qt. saucepan until done: 30 to 40 min. for whole potatoes; 20 to 25 min. for cut-up potatoes. When a fork pierces a potato easily, it is done. Drain excess cooking water. Using potato masher or electric mixer, mash hot potatoes thoroughly until no lumps remain. Gradually beat in hot milk (amount depends on kind of potatoes used), then butter and seasonings. Whip vigorously until light and fluffy. Serve immediately, topped with a lump of butter. *2 to 3 servings.*

Buttered Brussels Sprouts

Remove any loose or discolored leaves from ¾ lb. fresh Brussels sprouts. Cut off stem ends. Leave sprouts whole. Wash thoroughly in lukewarm water. Cook, uncovered, in boiling salted water until just tender, about 8 to 10 min. Serve at once, seasoned with pepper and a generous amount of melted butter. *2 servings.*

Pecan Tarts

Prepare ½ pie crust stick according to directions on inside wrapper, being careful to use just half the amount of liquid called for in a One-crust Pie. Line two 4″ tart pans with the pastry.

Heat oven to 375° (quick mod.). Pour Pecan Filling (below) into pastry-lined pans. Bake 40 to 50 min., until filling is set and pastry is nicely browned. Serve cold or slightly warm; garnish with whipped cream. *2 servings.*

Pecan Filling

1 egg	¼ cup plus 2 tbsp. dark corn syrup
¼ cup sugar	
⅛ tsp. salt	¼ cup plus 2 tbsp. pecan halves
2 tbsp. butter, melted	

Beat together with rotary beater all ingredients except pecans. Then mix in pecans.

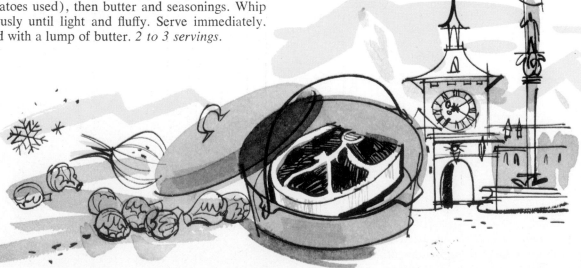

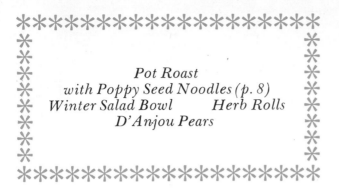

*Pot Roast
with Poppy Seed Noodles (p. 8)
Winter Salad Bowl   Herb Rolls
D'Anjou Pears*

Pot Roast

Select 2-lb. boneless chuck roast. Brown pot roast well in hot fat in Dutch oven or heavy kettle, 15 to 20 min. on each side. As each side is browned, salt and pepper generously. Set pot roast on low rack or on one improvised from jar lids punched with holes, to prevent burning. Add ½ cup water. Cover tightly and simmer over low heat 2½ to 3 hr., until fork tender. Check now and then and add only enough water to keep meat from sticking to kettle. About 45 min. before roast is done, add 2 to 4 small peeled onions and 4 to 5 medium carrots; sprinkle vegetables lightly with salt. Serve hot with Kettle Gravy (p. 121). *2 generous servings.*

Electric Skillet Pot Roast

Use same amount of meat and vegetables as for Pot Roast (above). Brown roast in electric skillet heated to 375°. After browning on all sides, season with salt and pepper. Lower heat to 225°. Place onions around meat; season with salt. Add no water. Keeping vent closed, cook covered 2 hr., or until meat is tender. One hr. before roast is done, add carrots; sprinkle lightly with salt. Serve hot with Pan Gravy (p. 121).

Winter Salad Bowl

½ cup grated raw
  parsnip (1 medium)
2 tbsp. chopped sweet
  onion
¼ cup chopped celery
4 pimiento-stuffed
  olives, chopped

¼ tsp. salt
French Dressing
  (p. 25)
⅓ medium head
  lettuce, torn into
  bite-sized pieces
2 tbsp. mayonnaise

Marinate first five ingredients in French Dressing for 1 or 2 hr. Just before serving, add lettuce. Toss lightly with mayonnaise. *2 to 3 servings.*

Note: The grated rind and sections of ½ orange may be used in place of the olives.

Herb Rolls

Brush tops of Brown 'N Serve Rolls with olive oil or butter before baking. Sprinkle lightly with herbs of your choice, such as dried or fresh thyme, sage, tarragon, or basil. Bake in 400° (mod. hot) oven 10 to 12 min.

D'Anjou Pears

4 d'Anjou pears
½ cup brown sugar
  (packed)
⅓ cup maple syrup
¼ cup water

dash of salt
dash of ginger
1½ tsp. grated
  lemon rind

Heat oven to 325° (slow mod.). Wash pears. Cut thin slice from blossom end so pears will stand easily. Leave stems on. Place pears upright in baking dish. Mix remaining ingredients and pour over pears. Bake uncovered about 1½ hr., or until pears are tender. Baste syrup over pears occasionally while baking. Serve 2 of the pears slightly warm with syrup. *4 servings.*

Leftover Pears? Refrigerate; serve chilled with garnish of whipped cream on the following day.

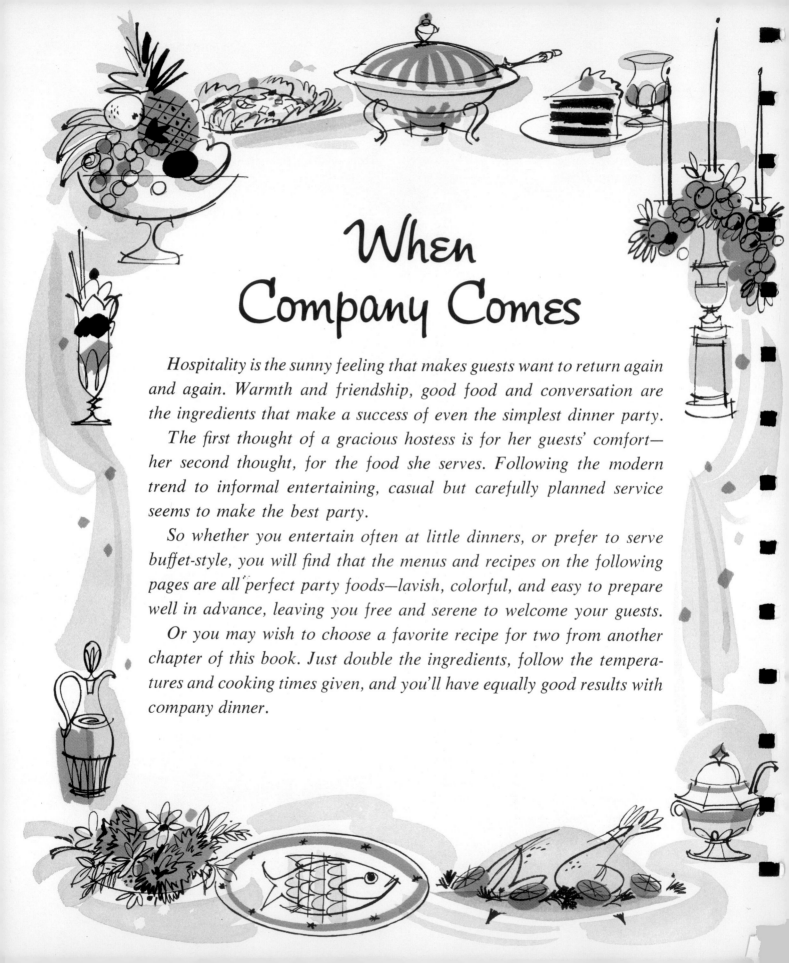

When Company Comes

Hospitality is the sunny feeling that makes guests want to return again and again. Warmth and friendship, good food and conversation are the ingredients that make a success of even the simplest dinner party.

The first thought of a gracious hostess is for her guests' comfort—her second thought, for the food she serves. Following the modern trend to informal entertaining, casual but carefully planned service seems to make the best party.

So whether you entertain often at little dinners, or prefer to serve buffet-style, you will find that the menus and recipes on the following pages are all perfect party foods—lavish, colorful, and easy to prepare well in advance, leaving you free and serene to welcome your guests.

Or you may wish to choose a favorite recipe for two from another chapter of this book. Just double the ingredients, follow the temperatures and cooking times given, and you'll have equally good results with company dinner.

Little Dinners for Saturday Night

A "little dinner" has its own elegance when the food is special like the following menus—and you serve it handsomely with your prettiest table setting.

Pheasant en Crème
Wild Rice
Sautéed Tomatoes
Orange-Bermuda Onion Salad (p. 9)
Caraway Bread Sticks
Cranberry-Apple Pie

Pheasant en Crème

1 pheasant, quartered (2 pheasants, if small)	¾ tsp. salt
	⅓ cup chopped onion
1 can (10½ oz.) cream of chicken soup	1 clove garlic, minced
½ cup apple cider	1 can (3 oz.) mushrooms
1 tbsp. plus 1 tsp. Worcestershire sauce	paprika

Heat oven to 350° (mod.). Place pheasant in square baking pan, 9x9x1¾" (for 2 pheasants, a 13x9½x2" baking pan and double amounts of remaining ingredients). Blend soup, cider, Worcestershire sauce, salt, onion, garlic, and mushrooms. Pour over pheasant. Sprinkle generously with paprika. Bake 1½ to 2 hr., or until tender. Baste with sauce during baking. After baking 1 hr., sprinkle again with paprika. *4 servings.*

Chicken en Crème

Make Pheasant en Crème (above)—except use a broiler-fryer chicken (2 lb.) instead of pheasant.

Wild Rice

Wash ½ cup wild rice in cold water. Cover with 2 cups boiling water. Cover and let stand 20 min. Drain and repeat 3 times, using fresh boiling water each time and adding 1½ tsp. salt the last time. Season with salt, pepper, and generous amount of butter. Rice may be kept warm in oven or in double boiler. (Cover if held longer than 5 min.) *4 servings.*

Sautéed Tomatoes

Dip firm tomato slices (¼" thick) into Seasoned Flour (p. 6), then into slightly beaten egg, then into fine cracker crumbs. Sprinkle with salt and pepper. Brown both sides in hot melted butter in heavy skillet, about 10 min.

Caraway Bread Sticks

1 cup warm water (not hot—110 to 115°)	1½ tsp. salt
	½ tsp. nutmeg
1 pkg. active dry yeast	1 tsp. leaf sage, crumbled
3 to 3¼ cups all-purpose flour	2 tsp. caraway seeds
1 tbsp. sugar	¼ cup soft shortening
	1 egg

Measure water into mixing bowl. Add yeast, stirring to dissolve. Measure flour by dipping method (p. 123) or by sifting. Stir into yeast mixture with remaining ingredients; beat vigorously. Cover and refrigerate at least 2 hr. or overnight before forming into sticks.

About 2 hr. before baking, divide chilled dough into 2 parts. Return half to refrigerator for use in several days. Divide remaining dough into 18 small pieces. Roll in 8" pencil-like strips; place 1" apart on greased baking sheet. Let rise until double, 1½ to 2 hr.

Heat oven to 400° (mod. hot). Bake 12 to 15 min., or until crisp and golden brown. *Makes 18 bread sticks.*

Leftover Bread Sticks? They're wonderful for snacks—and won't become stale because they're so crispy.

Cranberry-Apple Pie

Make Apple Pie (p. 59)—except substitute 1½ cups whole fresh or thawed frozen cranberries for 1½ cups of sliced apples, increase sugar to 1¼ cups, and mix 3 tbsp. flour with fruit, sugar, and spices.

*Sauerbraten
with Gingersnap Gravy
Potato Balls
Sweet-sour Red Cabbage
Pumpernickel Slices
Lemon Schaum Tortes*

Sauerbraten

Perfect for the larger dinner party.

4-lb. chuck roast	12 juniper berries,
2 onions, sliced	if desired
2 bay leaves	2 tsp. salt
6 whole cloves	1 pt. red wine vinegar
12 peppercorns	½ cup boiling water

Place roast in an earthenware bowl with onions and seasonings. Pour over it a mixture of red wine vinegar and boiling water. Marinate 3 days or more in refrigerator. Turn meat twice a day with 2 wooden spoons; never pierce with a fork.

To cook: drain meat and brown thoroughly on all sides in hot fat in heavy skillet. Add marinade; cover pan and simmer slowly 3 to 4 hr., or until tender. Serve meat with Gingersnap Gravy (below). *8 servings.*

Gingersnap Gravy

When meat is done, remove to platter. Pour off any excess fat. Add 2 tsp. sugar and 8 crumbled gingersnaps and cook 10 min. longer. Thicken with a flour-water paste (1 tbsp. flour per cup of liquid). Bring to boil; boil 1 min. Season and serve.

Sweet-sour Red Cabbage

1 medium head red	1¾ cups water
cabbage (about	½ cup mild vinegar
2 lb.)	1 tsp. sugar
1 small onion, diced	4 whole cloves
2 tbsp. shortening	salt and pepper to
1 apple, cut into	taste
quarters	2 tbsp. flour

Grate or slice cabbage into small pieces. Brown onion in shortening. Add all ingredients except flour. Cover; cook until cabbage is tender, about 30 to 35 min. Thicken with flour. *8 servings.*

Potato Balls

6 medium-sized	1 egg
potatoes	¼ cup plus 2 tbsp.
2 slices white bread	all-purpose flour
2 tbsp. butter	salt

Pare and cook potatoes. Mash while hot. Let cool. Cut bread into small cubes and toast in butter, melted in skillet, until golden brown. When potatoes are cool, blend in egg, flour, and salt to taste. Form potato mixture into 8 to 10 balls, placing three cubes of toasted bread in the center of each ball. Gently place the balls in boiling salted water and simmer 10 to 15 min. *8 to 10 potato balls.*

Lemon Schaum Tortes

Bake 8 individual Meringue Shells (below). Prepare Lemon Custard Filling (below) and cool. Whip 1 cup whipping cream until stiff.

Spread half the whipped cream over the cooled baked Meringue Shells. Cover with Lemon Custard Filling. Top with remaining cream. Chill in refrigerator at least 12 hr. *8 servings.*

Meringue Shells

4 egg whites	1⅓ cups sugar
¼ tsp. cream of tartar	

Beat egg whites until frothy. Add cream of tartar and continue beating until stiff enough to hold a point. Beat sugar in gradually, continuing beating until mixture is stiff and glossy and sugar is well blended.

Use this meringue to make 8 individual meringue shells; drop meringue for each on heavy brown paper on baking sheet. Shape into shells with back of spoon.

Heat oven to 275° (very slow). Bake 60 min. Turn off oven and leave in until cool.

Lemon Custard Filling

Beat 4 egg yolks until thick and lemon-colored. Beat ½ cup sugar in gradually. Blend in ¼ cup lemon juice and 2 tbsp. grated lemon rind. Cook over hot water until thickened (5 to 8 min.), stirring constantly. Cool.

Roast Cornish Game Hens
Cranberry-Orange Relish (p. 6)
Parisienne Potatoes
Buttered Broccoli
(double recipe on p. 62)
French Bread
Angel Food Cake
with Ice Cream and Strawberries

Roast Cornish Game Hens

For four servings, buy four 12- to 15-oz. frozen game hens. Thaw. Then wash hens and pat dry.

Heat oven to 425° (hot). Season thawed hens inside with salt and pepper. Roast without stuffing, or stuff each hen with 1½ to 2 tbsp. Bread Stuffing (p. 51). Place breast-side-up in roasting pan. Brush with melted butter. Roast about 1 hr., until fork tender, brushing hens with butter 2 or 3 times during roasting. Serve immediately.

Parisienne Potatoes

Roll cooked canned potato balls or small whole potatoes in hot melted butter. A 1-lb. can of cooked small whole potatoes is just right for four.

ANGEL FOOD CAKE
Bake a perfect high, light angel with angel food cake mix. Remaining slices keep beautifully for lunchboxes, picnics, and other desserts.

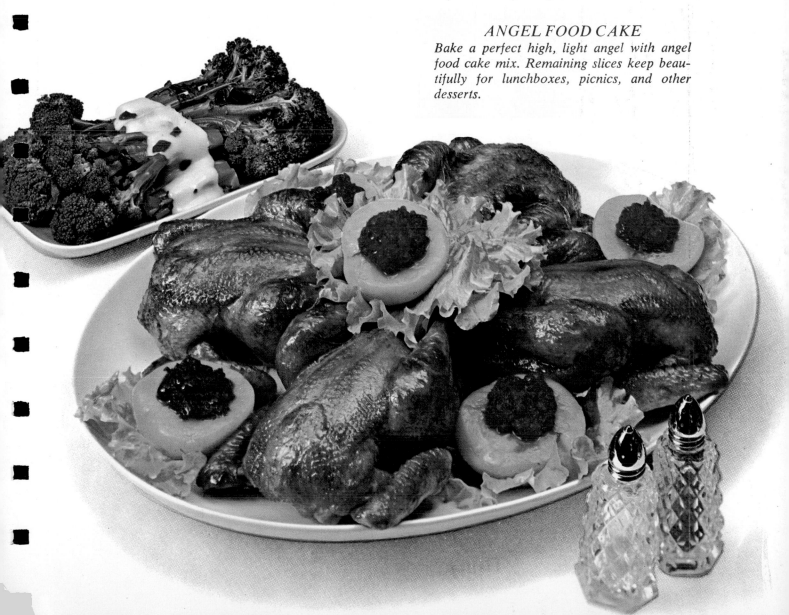

Mock Champagne
Savory Crackers
Chicken Breasts Baked in Cream
Wild Rice with Mushrooms and Almonds
Minted Peas (double recipe on p. 71)
Blushing Pear Salad
Hot Rolls
Pot de Crème au Chocolat

Mock Champagne

Combine equal amounts of chilled apple juice and ginger ale.

Savory Crackers

Brush saltine crackers with soft butter; sprinkle with poppy seeds, celery seeds, onion salt, or paprika. Heat in 300° (slow) oven 8 min. or until lightly browned.

Chicken Breasts Baked in Cream

Pheasant is also delicious cooked in this manner.

2 whole chicken breasts (about 2 lb.)	¾ cup cream (20% butterfat)
3 tbsp. shortening	1½ tsp. salt
⅓ cup chopped onion	⅛ tsp. pepper
1 small clove garlic, minced	2 tsp. Worcestershire sauce
¾ cup chicken broth	

Heat oven to 300° (slow). Cut chicken breasts in half crosswise, making four serving pieces. In a heavy skillet, brown breasts in shortening until golden. Add remaining ingredients. Cover tightly. Bake about 2 hr., or until tender. Just before serving, remove chicken from skillet; keep warm while making Pan Gravy (p. 121). *4 servings.*

Wild Rice with Mushrooms and Almonds

2 tbsp. butter	1 can (7 oz.) mushroom pieces and stems, drained
½ cup wild rice	
¼ cup blanched, slivered almonds	
1 tbsp. chopped green onion or chives	1½ cups chicken broth

Put all ingredients except broth in heavy frying pan; cook over medium high heat about 20 min., or until almonds are slightly brown. Stir often.

Heat oven to 300° (slow). When almonds are brown, add chicken broth to rest of ingredients; stir. Pour mixture into 1-qt. baking dish. Cover tightly and bake about 2 hr. *4 servings.*

Blushing Pear Salad

Prepare 1 pkg. (3 oz.) lime-flavored gelatin as directed on pkg. Tint 6 pear halves a soft pink with a solution of red food coloring and water. Arrange pear halves cut-side-down in square pan, 9x9x1¾". Pour gelatin into pan; surround pears. Chill until firm. Serve a pear half in gelatin on salad greens with Lime-ade Dressing (p. 82) on individual plates. *6 servings.*

Leftover Salad? Another day, serve remaining pear halves in gelatin in individual dessert dishes topped with whipped cream or Quick Custard Sauce (p. 14).

Pot de Crème au Chocolat

1 bar (4 oz.) sweet cooking chocolate	2 egg yolks, slightly beaten
1 tbsp. sugar	½ tsp. vanilla
½ cup cream	whipped cream

Mix chocolate, sugar, and cream in saucepan and heat over medium heat, stirring constantly, until chocolate melts and mixture becomes smooth and blended. Remove from heat. Slowly pour into egg yolks, stirring constantly. Blend in vanilla. Pour into small individual dessert dishes or demitasse cups. Chill. Garnish with whipped cream. *4 servings.*

Antipasto
Pizza
Lettuce or Spinach Salad
with Garlic Dressing
Biscuit Tortoni

Antipasto

Use your ingenuity to arrange attractively on a bed of endive or watercress (on individual plates or a platter) a tasty combination of any of the following:

pieces of tuna	celery stuffed with
radish slices	softened cheese
pickled beet cubes	artichoke hearts
pimiento-stuffed olives	curls of cooked ham
hard-cooked egg slices	slices of smoked pork
	small green peppers

Drizzle olive oil over all and sprinkle with salt and pepper to taste. Serve as an appetizer course with bread sticks or with garlic bread that has been toasted and sprinkled with Parmesan cheese.

Biscuit Tortoni

⅓ cup fine macaroon crumbs	¼ cup chopped salted almonds
2 tbsp. diced candied cherries	1 pt. vanilla ice cream

Combine all ingredients except ice cream. Turn temperature control of refrigerator to coldest setting. Slightly soften ice cream and fold in the macaroon-cherry-almond mixture. Spoon into ice cube tray or little paper cups in ice cube tray. Freeze until firm, then reset temperature control to normal. *4 servings.*

Pizza

2 cups buttermilk baking mix	1 cup grated Cheddar cheese
½ cup water	¾ lb. ground beef, browned
½ cup grated Parmesan cheese	½ cup chopped green pepper
1 can (8 oz.) tomato sauce	pepper to taste
	¼ cup chopped onion

Heat oven to 425° (hot). Mix baking mix and water. Knead about 1 min. on lightly floured surface. Roll out ¼″ thick into a circle. Place on ungreased baking sheet. Pinch edge of circle to make slight rim. Place remaining ingredients on dough in order listed above. Bake 20 to 25 min., or until crust is brown and filling hot and bubbly. Cut into wedges; serve immediately.

Quick Pizza: Make Pizza (above)—except use 1 cup sliced pepperoni or chopped salami.

Bits of Pizza: Make Pizza (above)—except roll out dough and cut into 3″ squares. Pinch edges of square to form rim. Fill with desired filling or have ingredients available for guests to make their own. *Makes about 12.*

Garlic Dressing

Prepare a double recipe of French Dressing, American Style (p. 25). Just before serving, mix in 1 clove garlic, crushed to a paste, and some freshly ground pepper.

Chicken, Pork, or Veal Chow Mein
Small Mounds of Fluffy White Rice
Soy Sauce
Mandarin Orange Sections
Little Chinese Almond Cakes

Chicken, Pork, or Veal Chow Mein

¼ cup vegetable oil	2 tsp. sugar
1 tsp. salt	2 cups chicken broth
¼ tsp. pepper	or water
2 cups sliced Chinese	2½ tbsp. cornstarch
cabbage	¼ cup water
3 cups thinly sliced	¼ cup soy sauce
celery	2 cups sliced cooked
1 can (1 lb.) bean	chicken, pork, or
sprouts, drained	veal, cut in thin
1 can (4 oz.) water	slivers
chestnuts, sliced	chow mein noodles

Heat oil, salt, and pepper in deep skillet. Add cabbage, celery, bean sprouts, water chestnuts, and sugar. Stir in chicken broth; cook about 10 min. Mix cornstarch, water, and soy sauce; add to vegetable mixture. Stir until mixture thickens. Add meat and heat through. Serve over hot chow mein noodles. *4 servings.*

Little Chinese Almond Cakes

Shortbread type. Perfect with fresh fruit or with orange ice to finish a chow mein supper.

1 cup all-purpose flour	½ tsp. almond extract
½ cup shortening	or vanilla
(half butter)	1 egg yolk
½ tsp. salt	1 tbsp. water
¼ cup plus 2 tbsp.	¼ cup blanched
sugar	almonds

Measure flour by dipping method (p. 123) or by sifting. Place flour in bowl; cut in shortening finely. Use hands to work in salt, sugar, and flavoring. Shape into long roll, 1″ in diameter; wrap in waxed paper. Chill about 1 hr. Heat oven to 400° (mod. hot). Cut roll into ¼″ slices. Place 1″ apart on lightly greased baking sheet. Brush each slice with a mixture of egg yolk and water. Press ½ blanched almond into top of each. Bake 8 to 10 min., or until light golden brown. *Makes about 2 doz. cakes.*

Veal à la Madelon
Parisienne Potatoes (p. 41)
Peas, French Style
Green Salad
(double recipe on p. 59)
Sour Cream and Chive Buns
Chocolate Eclairs
Demitasse

Veal à la Madelon

1 clove garlic, minced	1 tsp. salt
2 tbsp. butter	¼ tsp. pepper
2 lb. boneless veal, cut in bite-sized pieces	two 1″ wide strips lemon peel
2 tbsp. flour	1 cup boiling water
	1 cup whipping cream

Sauté garlic in hot butter in heavy skillet. Remove garlic and brown veal in the butter. Sprinkle flour, salt, and pepper over meat. Brown again. Add lemon peel and water. Cover. Simmer about 1 hr., or until tender. Remove lemon peel. Stir in cream. Heat through. Serve hot over Parisienne Potatoes (p. 41). *4 servings.*

Sour Cream and Chive Buns

¾ cup commercial sour cream	2¼ cups all-purpose flour
2 tbsp. sugar	1 egg
1 tsp. salt	1½ tbsp. chopped chives or fresh dill seeds
2 tbsp. soft shortening	
1 pkg. active dry yeast	
¼ cup warm water (not hot—110 to 115°)	

Mix sour cream, sugar, salt, and shortening. Bring just to boil; cool to lukewarm. In mixing bowl, dissolve yeast in warm water. Stir in sour cream mixture and half of flour. Beat with spoon until smooth. Add remaining flour, egg, and chives; beat until smooth. Scrape down sides of bowl. Cover with cloth and let rise in warm place (85°) until double in bulk, about 30 min. (If kitchen is cool, place dough on a rack over a bowl of hot water and cover completely with a towel.)

Grease 12 medium-sized muffin cups. Stir down batter. Spoon into cups, filling ½ full. Let rise in warm place until dough reaches tops of muffin cups, 20 to 30 min. Heat oven to 400° (mod. hot). Bake 15 to 20 min. *Makes 12 buns.*

Peas, French Style

lettuce leaves	½ tsp. salt
2 cups freshly shelled green peas or 1 pkg. (10 oz.) frozen peas	a dash each pepper, nutmeg, and sugar
	¼ cup butter

Line bottom and sides of heavy saucepan with washed lettuce leaves. Add peas. Sprinkle with salt, pepper, nutmeg, and sugar. Add butter. Cover with more lettuce leaves. Cook covered over low heat about 20 min., or until tender. Discard leaves. *4 servings.*

Chocolate Eclairs

½ cup water	Vanilla Custard Filling (below)
¼ cup butter	Thin Chocolate Icing (below)
½ cup all-purpose flour	
2 eggs	

Heat oven to 400° (mod. hot). Heat water and butter to rolling boil in saucepan. Measure flour by dipping method (p. 123) or by sifting. Stir in flour, stirring vigorously over low heat until mixture forms a ball (about 1 min.). Remove from heat. Beat in eggs thoroughly, one at a time. Beat until smooth. Shape with spatula into 6 fingers, each 4″ long and 1″ wide. Bake 45 to 50 min. or until puffed, golden brown, and dry. Cool slowly away from drafts. Cut off tops; scoop out filaments of soft dough. Fill 4 éclairs with Vanilla Custard Filling for immediate serving. Frost with Thin Chocolate Icing. *Makes 6 éclairs.*

Leftover Eclairs? Store them *unfilled* and serve the following day.

Vanilla Custard Filling

⅓ cup plus 1 tbsp. sugar	1½ cups milk
¼ cup plus 1 tbsp. all-purpose flour	2 egg yolks (or 1 whole egg), beaten
dash of salt	1½ tsp. vanilla or other flavoring

Mix sugar, flour, and salt in saucepan. Stir in milk. Cook over medium heat, stirring until it boils. Boil 1 min. Remove from heat. Stir a little over half of mixture into egg yolks. Blend into hot mixture in saucepan. Bring *just* to boil. Cool and blend in vanilla. *Fills 6 éclairs.*

Thin Chocolate Icing

½ sq. unsweetened chocolate (½ oz.)	½ cup confectioners' sugar
1 tsp. butter	1 tbsp. boiling water

Melt chocolate and butter over hot water. Remove from heat. Blend in sugar and water. Beat only until smooth but not stiff.

Buffet Suppers

A delightful, informal, and effortless dinner party can be given easily without extra help if you use buffet service. The food is all placed on the table at one time. Plates, silver, and napkins are arranged conveniently so that the guests may serve themselves. They may then take their plates to smaller tables set up nearby or in an adjoining room. Dessert may be served by the hostess and passed to the guests, or it may be set out with the coffee on either another table or the cleared buffet table, where each guest serves himself.

Hamburger Stroganoff
Poppy Seed Noodles
(double recipe on p. 8)
French-style Green Beans
(double recipe on p. 59)
Hot Buttered French Bread
Orange Slices and Dates on Endive
(with your favorite fruit salad dressing)
Chiffon Cake topped with Cocoa Fluff

Hamburger Stroganoff

½ cup minced onion	1 lb. fresh mushrooms,
1 clove garlic, minced	sliced, or 1 can (8 oz.)
¼ cup butter	sliced mushrooms,
1 lb. ground beef	drained
2 tbsp. flour	1 can (10½ oz.)
1 tsp. salt	cream of chicken
¼ tsp. pepper	soup, undiluted
	1 cup commercial
	sour cream
	parsley

Sauté onion and garlic in butter over medium heat. Stir in meat and brown. Stir in flour, salt, pepper, and mushrooms. Cook 5 min. Stir in soup. Simmer uncovered 10 min. Stir in sour cream. Heat through. Garnish with parsley. *4 to 6 servings.*

Serving Ideas: Arrange Poppy Seed Noodles in a ring; center with Hamburger Stroganoff. Or serve with Fluffy White Rice (double recipe on p. 26).

Hot Buttered French Bread

Slice bread diagonally, not quite through bottom crust. Spread with butter. Heat loaf until piping hot in a 400° (mod. hot) oven, about 15 min.

Chiffon Cake

1 cup plus 2 tbsp.	¼ cup plus 2 tbsp.
cake flour	cold water
¾ cup sugar	1 tsp. vanilla
1½ tsp. baking powder	1 tsp. grated lemon
½ tsp. salt	rind
¼ cup vegetable oil	½ cup egg whites (4)
2 egg yolks	¼ tsp. cream of
	tartar

Heat oven (see temperature below). Use a loaf pan, 9x5x3″, or a square pan, 8x8x2″ or 9x9x1¾″. Do not grease pans!

Spoon flour into nested dry measuring cup; level off with straight-edged spatula, or sift. Blend flour, sugar, baking powder, and salt in bowl. Make a well and add in order: oil, egg yolks, water, vanilla, and lemon rind. Beat with spoon until smooth. Measure egg whites and cream of tartar into large mixer bowl. Beat until whites form very stiff peaks. Pour egg yolk mixture gradually over beaten whites, gently folding with rubber scraper just until blended. Pour into ungreased pan. Bake loaf cake at 325° (slow mod.) for 50 to 55 min.; bake square cake at 350° (mod.) for 30 to 35 min., until top springs back when touched lightly. Invert, supporting pan on clip clothespins, until cool.

Note: If you substitute all-purpose flour for cake flour, measure flour by dipping method (p. 123) or by sifting and decrease amount of flour to 1 cup. Use 3 egg yolks.

ORANGE CHIFFON CAKE

Fluffy and light like angel food, yet rich and moist as butter cake. Now quickly and easily made with chiffon cake mix.

Cocoa Fluff

Mix in chilled bowl: 1 cup whipping cream, ½ cup sifted confectioners' sugar, and ¼ cup cocoa. Beat until stiff.

Ham Loaf

¾ lb. smoked ham,
  ground
¼ lb. fresh pork,
  ground
1 egg, beaten

½ cup milk
½ cup fine bread
  crumbs
⅛ tsp. pepper

Heat oven to 350° (mod.). Mix all ingredients thoroughly. Shape in 2 loaves in shallow baking pan. Bake 1 hr., or until done. *4 servings.*

Individual Ham Loaves

Make Ham Loaf (above)—except bake ham mixture in four tiny loaf pans, 4¾ x 2⅝ x 1½″. Bake in 350° oven 40 min. *4 servings.*

Note: Those cooking for one will find it handy to have Individual Ham Loaves and Twice-baked Potatoes in the freezer. Thaw and heat in 450° oven 30 min.

Individual Ham Loaves
Twice-baked Potatoes (p. 61)
Chinese-style Cabbage
Easy Pineapple Salad
Cinnamon Nut Cake

Chinese-style Cabbage

1 tbsp. shortening	1 medium onion,
3 cups finely shredded	chopped
cabbage	1 tsp. salt
1 cup chopped celery	⅛ tsp. pepper
1 medium green	
pepper, chopped	

Heat shortening in skillet. Drop in vegetables; stir well. Cover tightly. Steam 5 min. on medium heat, stirring several times. Season with salt and pepper. Serve immediately. *4 servings.*

Easy Pineapple Salad

1 pkg. (3 oz.) cream	4 pineapple slices
cheese	lettuce
1 tbsp. pineapple juice	green grapes

Blend cream cheese and pineapple juice. Spread pineapple slices with cheese mixture. Place on lettuce. Garnish with green grapes. *Makes 4 individual salads.*

Cinnamon Nut Cake

⅓ cup soft butter or	1 tsp. baking powder
margarine	1 tbsp. cinnamon
1 cup sugar	⅓ cup milk
2 eggs	⅔ cup broken nuts
1 cup all-purpose flour	

Heat oven to 350° (mod.). Grease and flour a square pan, 8x8x2″. Mix butter, sugar, and eggs in mixing bowl. Beat 5 min., high speed on mixer or by hand. Measure flour by dipping method (p. 123) or by sifting. Blend flour, baking powder, and cinnamon. Add alternately in three additions with milk, starting and ending with dry ingredients. Beat on low speed *just* until smooth; fold in nuts. Pour into prepared pan. Bake 35 to 40 min. Frost half of cake with Browned Butter Icing (p. 35); freeze remaining half for later use.

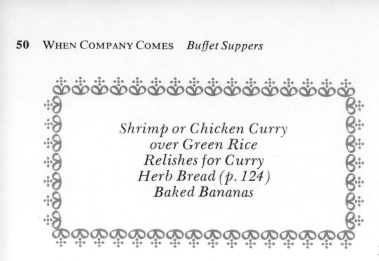

*Shrimp or Chicken Curry
over Green Rice
Relishes for Curry
Herb Bread (p. 124)
Baked Bananas*

Shrimp or Chicken Curry

¼ cup plus 2 tbsp. butter	2 cups chicken broth (or 2 chicken bouillon cubes dissolved in 2 cups hot water)
½ cup minced onion	
1 tbsp. curry powder	
¼ cup plus 2 tbsp. all-purpose flour	
1½ tsp. salt	2 cups milk
1½ tsp. sugar	4 cups cooked, cleaned shrimp or cut-up cooked chicken
¼ tsp. ground ginger	
	1 tsp. lemon juice

Melt butter over low heat in heavy saucepan. Sauté onion and curry powder in melted butter. Blend in flour and seasonings. Cook over low heat until mixture is smooth and bubbly; remove from heat. Stir in chicken broth and milk. Bring to a boil, stirring constantly. Boil 1 min. Add shrimp or chicken and lemon juice. Heat. *8 servings.*

TO SERVE CURRY

Each person helps himself to Green Rice (below), spoons shrimp or chicken curry over the rice, then sprinkles over the top at least 6 relishes in desired amount.

Green Rice

3 cups cooked white rice	1¼ tsp. salt
1 cup chopped spinach or parsley or combination	½ tbsp. grated onion or scant ¼ tsp. onion powder
2 eggs, well beaten	¼ cup butter, melted
1 cup milk	½ cup grated sharp cheese
1 tsp. Worcestershire sauce	

Heat oven to 325° (slow mod.). Toss rice and spinach together. Add eggs, milk, Worcestershire sauce, salt, and onion. Pour into 10x6x1½″ oblong baking dish or 2-qt. baking dish. Sprinkle butter and cheese over rice. Bake 30 to 40 min. *8 servings.*

Relishes for Curry

Raisins	Sweet or sour pickles
Salted almonds	
Salted peanuts	Currant jelly
Sautéed onion rings	Flaked coconut
Pineapple chunks	India relish
Chopped hard-cooked eggs	Sliced avocado
Crisp bacon bits	Chutney

Baked Bananas

Heat oven to 375° (quick mod.). Split 4 large bananas lengthwise; place in greased baking dish. To prepare each banana (2 halves): brush with about 1½ tsp. lemon juice, sprinkle with 1 tsp. lemon rind and 1 tbsp. brown sugar, drizzle with 1 tbsp. melted butter. Bake 20 min. Serve warm, plain or with ice cream. *8 servings.*

Holiday Dinners

What better way to celebrate than sharing a holiday meal with friends you hold near and dear. Set the table with your finest china and silver—and use your imagination to create a distinctive holiday centerpiece.

Spiced Cider
Roast Chicken or Turkey
Bread Stuffing   Pan Gravy (p. 121)
Cranberry Sauce   Creamed Onions
Candied Sweet Potatoes
Celery Sticks   Holiday Breads
Mince Pie (p. 115)

Roast Chicken or Turkey

Select roasting chicken or young turkey. Allow ½ to ¾ lb. ready-to-cook weight for each serving. Remove any pin feathers and wash. Pat dry. Place stuffing in poultry *just before* roasting. Make 1 cup stuffing for each ready-to-cook lb. of poultry. Stuff body and neck cavities lightly. Stuffing should never be packed in.

Tie leg ends to tail or push them under band of skin at tail, if present. Skewer neck skin to back. Fold wings across back with tips touching. Rub skin with unsalted fat.

Heat oven (see chart below). Place poultry, breast-up, on rack in shallow roasting pan. Do not sear. Do not add water. Do not cover. Place in oven. When turkey is two-thirds done, cut cord or band of skin at drumsticks. Cover turkey loosely with tent of heavy-duty aluminum foil to prevent excessive browning.

Roast until done (leg joint should move readily).

Ready-to-Cook Weight	Oven Temperature	Approximate Cooking Time
Turkey		
6 to 8 lb.	325°	3 to 3½ hr.
8 to 12 lb.	325°	3½ to 4½ hr.
Chicken		
2½ to 3 lb.	375°	1½ to 1¾ hr.
3 to 4 lb.	375°	1¾ to 2 hr.

Bread Stuffing

⅓ cup butter	1 tsp. salt
¼ cup finely minced onion	¼ tsp. pepper
4 cups (1 qt.) coarse or fine bread crumbs or cubes	1 tsp. dried sage, thyme, or marjoram
½ cup chopped celery (stalks and leaves)	poultry seasoning to taste

Melt butter in large heavy skillet. Add onion and cook until yellow, stirring occasionally. Stir in some of bread crumbs. Heat, stirring to prevent excessive browning. Turn into deep bowl. Mix remaining ingredients and rest of bread crumbs lightly. For dry stuffing, add little or no liquid; for moist stuffing, mix in just enough hot water to moisten crumbs. *1 qt. makes enough stuffing for a 4-lb. fowl.*

Creamed Onions

Wash and peel 1½ lb. small dry onions. Leave whole. Cook, covered, in 1″ boiling salted water 15 to 20 min. Drain. Cover with 1 cup well-seasoned Medium White Sauce (p. 122). *4 servings.*

Candied Sweet Potatoes

1 cup brown sugar (packed)	½ tsp. salt
¼ cup butter	4 canned sweet potatoes
¼ cup water	

Mix sugar, butter, water, and salt in heavy skillet. Cook until mixture bubbles. Add potatoes and cook slowly, turning occasionally, until potatoes are glazed, about 20 min. *4 servings.*

Outdoor Entertaining

Following the trend to casual entertaining, more and more Americans are giving al fresco dinner parties during the warm-weather months. On these pages we suggest foods that are perfect for such occasions—easy to prepare and simple to serve.

Barbecued Spareribs
Stuffed Acorn Squash
Cucumber Sticks
Onion Butter Biscuits
Melon Sundaes

Barbecued Spareribs

4 lb. ribs, cut in serving pieces	1½ tbsp. cornstarch
3 cups water	barbecue sauce of your choice
½ cup soy sauce	

Place ribs and water in a large kettle with a cover. Bring to a boil; cook 5 min. Remove ribs from water; drain well. Place ribs in shallow glass dish; brush with a mixture of soy sauce and cornstarch. Cover dish; refrigerate 1 hr., turning meat occasionally. Place ribs bone-side-down on grill about 3″ from medium coals. Cook 30 min.; turn and cook 30 to 40 min. longer, turning and basting frequently with Sweet and Sour Sauce (below) or Texas Barbecue Sauce (right). Serve immediately with remaining sauce. *4 servings.*

Sweet and Sour Sauce

1 cup catsup	1 tbsp. celery seeds
1 cup water	1 tsp. chili powder
¼ cup brown sugar	1 tsp. salt
¼ cup Worcestershire sauce	⅛ tsp. pepper
¼ cup vinegar	few drops of red pepper sauce

Mix ingredients in saucepan; bring to boil. Use as basting sauce and serve remainder in individual dishes as a dip for barbecued ribs. *Makes 2¼ cups.*

Texas Barbecue Sauce

1 cup tomato juice	1 tbsp. paprika
½ cup water	1 tsp. dry mustard
¼ cup catsup	1 tsp. salt
¼ cup vinegar	¼ tsp. chili powder
2 tbsp. Worcestershire sauce	⅛ tsp. cayenne pepper
2 tbsp. brown sugar	

Mix ingredients in saucepan; simmer 15 min., or until slightly thickened. *Makes 2 cups.*

Stuffed Acorn Squash

Cut two acorn squash in half; remove the seeds. Place each half on a double thickness of heavy-duty aluminum foil. Put 1 tsp. butter and 2 tbsp. brown sugar in each half; add mixture of ¾ cup chopped apple and 2 tbsp. chopped walnuts. Dot with 2 tsp. butter and wrap securely in foil.

Barbecue on grill about 1 hr., turning once. Squash is done when it feels soft when touched with an asbestos-gloved thumb. *4 servings.*

Cucumber Sticks

Pare cucumber, cut in finger-like sticks. Chill thoroughly.

Onion Butter Biscuits

Melt 2 tbsp. plus 2 tsp. butter in small metal pie pan on grill. Add 1 tbsp. dehydrated onion soup mix. Spoon half of mixture into another pie pan. Make Biscuit dough as directed on buttermilk baking mix pkg.—except use ½ the amounts of ingredients, and add 1 tbsp. dehydrated onion soup mix to baking mix. Drop small biscuits into hot pie pan. Top with remaining butter mixture. Cover with other pie pan. Fry 8 to 10 min. on each side. *Makes 10 biscuits.*

Melon Sundaes

For each serving, place a scoop of vanilla ice cream in chilled melon half or alongside wedge.

Grilled Ham Slice
Roasted Sweet Potatoes
Old-fashioned Cabbage Salad
Corn Muffins from the Grill
Fresh Berries
Chocolate Chip Cookies

Grilled Ham Slice

Buy 1 lb. precooked ham steak or slice, cut about 1″ thick. Place on slightly greased grill over hot coals. Baste frequently with heated Chef's Special Sauce (below). Grill 5 to 7 min. per side, until steak is rich brown color and heated through. Serve remaining sauce with ham. *4 servings.*

Chef's Special Sauce

¼ cup prepared mustard	2 tbsp. sugar
¼ cup pineapple juice	½ tsp. horseradish
	dash of salt

Mix ingredients and heat. *Makes ½ cup.*

Roasted Sweet Potatoes

Rub 2 scrubbed sweet potatoes or yams with oil or butter and prick with fork. Wrap in heavy foil. Place on grill over hot coals. Bake, turning occasionally, about 1 hr., until tender. Unwrap; split lengthwise. Season with butter, salt, and pepper. *4 servings.*

Old-fashioned Cabbage Salad

1 tsp. salt	1 tbsp. plus 1 tsp. chopped red pepper or pimiento
¼ tsp. pepper	
½ tsp. dry mustard	
½ to 1 tsp. celery seeds	½ tsp. grated onion
	¼ cup vegetable oil
2 tbsp. sugar	⅓ cup white vinegar
¼ cup chopped green pepper	3 cups finely chopped cabbage

Place ingredients in large bowl in order given. Mix well. Cover and chill thoroughly. Garnish with watercress and sliced stuffed olives just before serving. *4 servings.*

Corn Muffins from the Grill

Bake Corn Muffins (p. 80) ahead of time. Split and butter generously. Wrap in double thickness of heavy-duty aluminum foil. Heat on grill over hot coals 10 min., turning once. Be careful—bread burns quickly!

Chocolate Chip Cookies

½ cup soft butter	½ cup chopped nuts
1 cup brown sugar (packed)	1 pkg. (6 oz.) semi-sweet chocolate pieces
1 egg	
2 cups buttermilk baking mix	

Heat oven to 375° (quick mod.). Mix butter, sugar, and egg well. Stir in baking mix, nuts, and chocolate pieces. Drop by teaspoonfuls about 2″ apart on ungreased baking sheet. Bake about 10 min., until lightly browned. *Makes 4 doz. 1½″ cookies.*

When Company Comes–Unexpectedly

Unexpected guests should be a pleasure, not a problem. And good hostesses are always prepared for off-the-cuff entertaining. They have a secret weapon—the well-planned emergency shelf, stocked with inspirations for just such occasions. These menus and recipes are planned for instant hospitality—complete and satisfying meals from foods you can always have on hand.

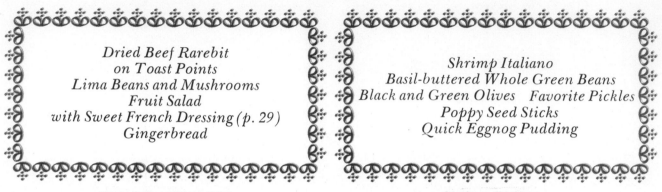

Dried Beef Rarebit
on Toast Points
Lima Beans and Mushrooms
Fruit Salad
with Sweet French Dressing *(p. 29)*
Gingerbread

Shrimp Italiano
Basil-buttered Whole Green Beans
Black and Green Olives   Favorite Pickles
Poppy Seed Sticks
Quick Eggnog Pudding

Dried Beef Rarebit

1 can (4 oz.) dried beef, shredded	1 tsp. dry mustard
water	½ tsp. paprika
¼ cup butter	2 cups milk
¼ cup all-purpose flour	1 cup grated sharp Cheddar cheese

If dried beef is very salty, cover with water; bring to a boil. Drain. Sauté beef in butter until edges curl. Blend in dry ingredients. Cook over low heat, stirring until mixture is smooth and bubbly. Remove from heat; stir in milk. Bring to a boil, stirring constantly; boil 1 min. Remove from heat; blend in cheese. Serve over toast points or toasted English muffins. *4 servings.*

Lima Beans and Mushrooms

Heat 1 can (16 oz.) Lima beans with 1 can (2 oz.) mushrooms. Drain. *4 servings.*

Fruit Salad

Drain 1 jar (1 lb. 13 oz.) or 1 can (1 lb.) fruits for salad. Add any fresh fruits you may have in the refrigerator. Serve in a lettuce-lined bowl; pass Sweet French Dressing (p. 29).

Shrimp Italiano

Make 1 pkg. (6 oz.) noodles Italiano as directed for oven-method—except add 1 can (4½ oz.) shrimp, drained, and 1 can (3 or 4 oz.) mushroom stems and pieces, drained, to noodles before layering in dish. *4 servings.*

Basil-buttered Whole Green Beans

Heat 1 can (15½ oz.) whole green beans; drain. Add 2 tbsp. butter and a pinch of basil. Toss lightly. *4 servings.*

Poppy Seed Sticks

Heat oven to 350° (mod.). Butter 2 or 3 slices of bread on both sides. Cut each slice into 6 equal strips. Place on baking sheet. Sprinkle with poppy seeds. Bake until crisp, turning sticks to brown both sides.

Quick Eggnog Pudding

Prepare 1 pkg. instant vanilla pudding as directed, adding 1 to 1½ tsp. brandy flavoring. Pour into dessert dishes; dash generously with nutmeg. *4 servings.*

FROM THE EMERGENCY SHELF
One 4-oz. can dried beef, 4-oz. pkg. grated sharp Cheddar cheese, 16-oz. can Lima beans, 2-oz. can mushrooms, 1-lb. 13-oz. jar or 1-lb. can fruits for salad, 14.5-oz. pkg. gingerbread mix.

FROM THE EMERGENCY SHELF
One 6-oz. pkg. noodles Italiano, 4½-oz. can shrimp, 3- or 4-oz. can mushrooms, 15½-oz. can whole green beans, small jar green olives, small jar black (ripe) olives, small jar favorite pickles (dill, sweet, watermelon), 1 pkg. instant vanilla pudding.

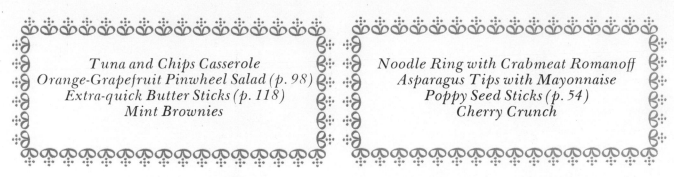

Tuna and Chips Casserole
Orange-Grapefruit Pinwheel Salad (p. 98)
Extra-quick Butter Sticks (p. 118)
Mint Brownies

Noodle Ring with Crabmeat Romanoff
Asparagus Tips with Mayonnaise
Poppy Seed Sticks (p. 54)
Cherry Crunch

Tuna and Chips Casserole

2 cans (10½ oz. each) cream of mushroom soup	2½ cups crushed potato chips
1 cup milk	2 cups (1 lb. can) cooked green peas, drained
2 cans (7 oz. each) tuna, drained and flaked	

Heat oven to 350° (mod.). Empty soup into 2-qt. baking dish. Add milk and mix well. Add tuna, 2 cups potato chips, and peas; mix lightly. Sprinkle remaining potato chips over top. Bake 25 min., until heated through. *6 to 8 servings.*

Planned-over Meal? This dish, reheated the next day, tastes just as good.

Chicken and Chips Casserole

Make Tuna and Chips Casserole (above)—except substitute cream of chicken soup for mushroom soup and use 2 cups cubed cooked chicken for the tuna.

Mint Brownies

Prepare batter using 1 pkg. (15.5 oz.) regular fudge brownie mix adding ¼ tsp. peppermint flavoring.

FROM THE EMERGENCY SHELF
Two 10½-oz. cans cream of mushroom soup, two 7-oz. cans tuna (or other seafood or meat), 1-lb. can green peas, 11-oz. can mandarin oranges, 11-oz. can grapefruit sections or 16-oz. can orange and grapefruit sections, 15.5-oz. pkg. fudge brownie mix.

Noodle Ring with Crabmeat Romanoff

Heat oven to 350° (mod.). Cook noodles as directed on 1 pkg. (5.5 oz.) noodles Romanoff. Drain. Blend in ¼ cup of dry sauce mix and ¼ cup milk. Add ¼ cup chopped parsley. Lightly pack into well-buttered 1-qt. ring mold. Set in pan of water (1" deep). Bake 15 min. Unmold; fill center with Crabmeat Romanoff (below). Garnish with parsley. *4 servings.*

Crabmeat Romanoff: Sauté 1 can (2 oz.) mushrooms, drained, in 2 tbsp. butter. Add ⅔ cup milk; bring to boil. Add rest of dry sauce mix; stir until smooth. Add 1 can (6½ oz.) crabmeat (all shell and cartilage removed); heat through.

Asparagus Tips with Mayonnaise

Drain 1 can (1 lb.) asparagus tips; chill uncovered. Just before serving, top with mayonnaise which has been thinned slightly with milk or cream. If you have greens on hand, serve asparagus on greens or in bowl lined with greens. *4 servings.*

Cherry Crunch

Heat oven to 350° (mod.). Cut ¼ cup butter into ½ pkg. (18.5-oz. size) yellow cake mix. Reserve ½ cup mixture. Pat remaining mixture lightly in a square pan, 8x8x2" or 9x9x1¾", building up ½" edge. Spread 1 can (1 lb. 4 oz.) cherry pie filling over cake mixture to within ½" of edge. Blend ¼ cup chopped walnuts and the ½ cup reserved mixture; sprinkle over cherries. Bake 35 to 40 min. Serve warm with whipped cream or ice cream. *8 servings.*

FROM THE EMERGENCY SHELF
One 5.5-oz. pkg. noodles Romanoff, 6½-oz. can crabmeat, 2-oz. can mushrooms, 1-lb. can asparagus tips, 18.5-oz. pkg. yellow cake mix, 1-lb. 4-oz. can cherry pie filling.

Variety–The Spice of Any Dinner

Make dinnertime a party every evening by the simple magic of a change of scene, a small addition to the menu, bright garnishes, or serving after-dinner coffee in the living room.

Switch the scene—Sometimes serve dinner on trays before the TV set, at a low table beside the living room fire—or on a summer evening, move to the patio, pack a picnic, set up a card table on the porch.

Change the setting—Collect colorful, inexpensive place mats and tablecloths in refreshing designs and tints.

Please the eye—Dine often by flattering candlelight; create an effective centerpiece of a few flowers or a pretty house plant arranged with a figurine or a favorite piece of pottery or silver.

Begin with a separate course—Start the meal with one of these: tomato juice spiced with red pepper sauce and Worcestershire sauce, served with a wedge of lemon and crisp crackers; a mug of hot consommé or clam juice; a small, chilled sea food or fruit cocktail; the salad planned for the meal.

Add a fancy bread—Serve hot muffins made from a mix or bake brown 'n serve rolls or refrigerated biscuits. But first brush them with melted butter and sprinkle with garlic or onion salt, chopped chives, or dried parsley flakes.

Add a special item to the menu—A special imported mustard, crisp watermelon pickles, a spiced peach or crabapple can dress up a simple meal. Serve chutney, a relish, guava or cherry jam, or a mixture of two jams such as apricot and pineapple. Add a relish tray of crisp, chilled celery and carrot sticks, cauliflower and broccoli buds, cottage cheese, cherry tomatoes, and olives.

Match beverages to the weather—On hot summer evenings, serve iced tea, iced coffee, or lemonade in place of hot coffee.

Serve after-dinner coffee—Demitasse, double-strength black coffee served hot in small after-dinner coffee cups; Vienna Coffee, demitasse topped with whipped cream and served with a cinnamon stick in place of a spoon; South American Coffee, equal parts of hot chocolate and black coffee.

Finish dinner with a dessert to linger over—Fresh fruit and a cheese tray with crisp, toasted crackers (bring cheeses to room temperature before serving and select contrasting varieties like aged Cheddar, a wedge of Bleu cheese, ripe Camembert, or Gruyère). Fresh strawberries to be dipped by their stems in brown sugar and sour cream. For special occasions, a chiffon or angel food cake on a plate surrounded with fresh flowers.

Two's Company

A birthday or anniversary, a raise in pay or a holiday far from family and friends—these are only a few of the many special dates or shared triumphs that call for celebration with a dinner party just for two. Choose a "company best" menu and serve it with all the gracious little touches you would add for guests —fine linen, silver, crystal, and an appropriate centerpiece.

Shrimp de Jonghe
Peas with Almonds
Fruit Cream Cheese Salad
Hard-crusted Rolls
Individual Brownie Alaskas

Shrimp de Jonghe

1 pkg. (7 oz.) frozen cleaned, uncooked shrimp	½ tsp. salt
1 clove garlic, sliced	2 tbsp. consommé or cooking sherry
¼ cup butter	¼ cup dry bread crumbs
dash each of tarragon, nutmeg, mace, thyme, pepper, and onion powder	1 tbsp. minced parsley

Heat oven to 400° (mod. hot). Cook 12 to 16 shrimp as directed on pkg. Do not overcook. (Do not thaw remaining shrimp. Make into shrimp cocktail or salad another day.) Drain cooked shrimp; place in 2 individual baking dishes. Cook garlic in butter until butter browns; remove garlic. Add herbs, seasonings, and consommé to butter. Remove 1 tbsp. butter mixture and toss with bread crumbs. Pour remaining butter mixture over shrimp. Top with buttered crumbs. Sprinkle with minced parsley. Bake 15 min. *2 servings.*

Peas with Almonds

Prepare and cook fresh peas as directed on p. 6 or cook frozen peas as directed on pkg. Serve garnished with slivered almonds. *2 servings.*

Fruit Cream Cheese Salad

For each serving, arrange pear or peach half or pineapple slice on salad greens. Garnish with cream cheese (about 1 tsp.) pressed through a fine sieve.

Individual Brownie Alaskas

For variety, try mint, strawberry, or pistachio ice cream. Brownies may be baked ahead of time, but make Alaskas just before serving.

Bake Brownies as directed on 1 pkg. (15.5 oz.) regular fudge brownie mix or in recipe, p. 20. Cut two 3x2¼″ pieces (use rest of Brownies as cookies). Make meringue by beating 1 egg white until stiff; add 2 tbsp. sugar gradually and continue beating until stiff and glossy. Place Brownie pieces on baking sheet covered with double thickness of aluminum foil. Top each piece with a slice of hard brick vanilla ice cream. Cover with meringue, being certain it completely covers ice cream and comes down to foil. Bake at 450° (hot) for 4 to 5 min., or until lightly browned. *2 servings.*

Broiled Steak
Baked "French Fried" Potatoes
Buttered Green Beans
Green Salad
with Oil-and-Vinegar Dressing
Hot Buttered French Bread (p. 46)
Apple Pie with Cheese

Broiled Steak

Allow ⅓ to ¾ lb. with bone or ⅓ to ½ lb. boneless for each serving.

Choose:
Club	**Sirloin**
Porterhouse	**Tenderloin**

Prepare steak for broiling by slashing through outside fat every inch or so to prevent meat from curling during broiling. Set oven regulator at "broil" or 550°. Place steak on rack in broiler pan so that the top surface is about 2″ from heat. (Close door on gas range; leave it ajar on electric range.)

Broil top side specified time (see below); season broiled side with salt and pepper. Turn meat with kitchen tongs. Broil other side; season. Serve immediately on hot platter.

	1″ thick	2″ thick
Rare:	5 min. each side	16 min. each side
Medium:	6 min. each side	18 min. each side
Well Done:	8 min. each side	20 min. each side

Baked "French Fried" Potatoes

Bake these before you start steak. When done, place below broiler tray in oven to keep warm while steak is broiled.

Melt fat in shallow pan. Pare 2 or 3 medium potatoes and cut in thin strips. Arrange in single layer in pan. Brush with melted fat. Bake in 425° (hot) oven 30 to 40 min. or 350° (mod.) oven 45 to 60 min., until tender. Turn occasionally. Season with salt and pepper before serving. *2 servings.*

Green Salad

Use 2 cups crisp, cold salad greens, torn into bite-sized pieces. (Try a variety of greens—head lettuce, leaf lettuce, endive, spinach, etc.) Toss with Oil-and-Vinegar Dressing (right) or other favorite dressing and serve immediately. *2 servings.*

Oil-and-Vinegar Dressing

2 tbsp. vegetable oil	ground fresh pepper
1 tbsp. vinegar	dash of flavor
¾ tsp. salt	enhancer (mono-
½ clove garlic, minced	sodium glutamate)

Toss oil with greens until leaves glisten. Mix vinegar and seasonings and toss sparingly in salad.

Quick Oil-and-Vinegar Dressing: Shake all ingredients together in a bottle.

Buttered Green Beans

Wash and snap ends off ¾ lb. fresh green beans. Leave whole, cut French-style into lengthwise strips, or cut crosswise into 1″ lengths. Cook, covered, in ½ to 1″ boiling salted water; whole beans, 15 to 20 min.; cut, 15 to 20 min.; French-style, 10 min. *2 servings.*

To save time, use 1 can (8 oz.) or 1 pkg. (10 oz.) frozen beans. Cook as directed.

Apple Pie

Tender-flaky Pastry for	¾ tsp. cinnamon or
8″ Two-crust Pie	nutmeg
(p. 126)	4 to 5 cups sliced
½ to ¾ cup sugar	pared apples
3 tbsp. flour	1 tbsp. butter

Heat oven to 425° (hot). Mix sugar, flour, spice; mix lightly through apples. Heap into pastry-lined pie pan. Dot with butter. Cover with top crust which has slits cut in it; seal and flute. Bake 50 to 60 min., until crust is browned and apples are cooked.

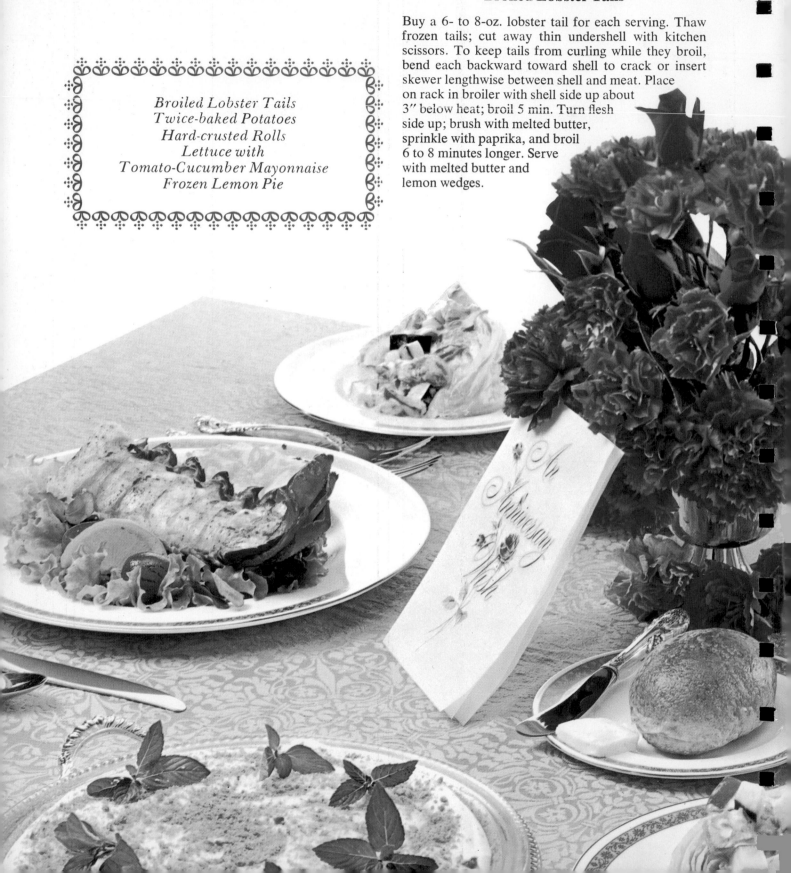

Broiled Lobster Tails
Twice-baked Potatoes
Hard-crusted Rolls
Lettuce with
Tomato-Cucumber Mayonnaise
Frozen Lemon Pie

Broiled Lobster Tails

Buy a 6- to 8-oz. lobster tail for each serving. Thaw frozen tails; cut away thin undershell with kitchen scissors. To keep tails from curling while they broil, bend each backward toward shell to crack or insert skewer lengthwise between shell and meat. Place on rack in broiler with shell side up about 3″ below heat; broil 5 min. Turn flesh side up; brush with melted butter, sprinkle with paprika, and broil 6 to 8 minutes longer. Serve with melted butter and lemon wedges.

Twice-baked Potatoes

Cut baked potatoes in half lengthwise. Scoop out potato; whip until fluffy with butter, milk, salt, and pepper. Mound back into shells. Sprinkle with paprika or grated cheese. Heat in 350° (mod.) oven 30 min. or in 400° (mod. hot) oven 20 to 25 min., until golden brown.

Note: Bake these before you start broiling. When done, place below broiler tray in oven to keep warm while lobster tails are broiled.

Tomato-Cucumber Mayonnaise

Fold ¼ cup each drained, diced tomato and cucumber, ½ tsp. minced onion, and salt into ½ cup mayonnaise. Serve over lettuce. *Makes 1 cup.*

Frozen Lemon Pie

½ cup fine graham cracker crumbs	1 cup whipping cream
3 eggs, separated	2 tsp. grated lemon rind
½ cup sugar	¼ cup lemon juice

Sprinkle half of crumbs in well-greased 9″ pie pan. Beat egg whites until frothy; gradually add sugar. Beat until stiff and glossy. Beat egg yolks until thick and lemon-colored; fold into egg-white mixture. Whip cream until stiff. Fold in lemon rind and juice. Fold into egg mixture. Pour into crumb-lined pie pan. Sprinkle rest of crumbs over top. Freeze. Remove from freezer 5 to 10 min. before serving.

Cheese Soufflé with Seafood Sauce
Buttered Broccoli
Green Salad (p. 59) with Chopped Olives
Dinner Rolls
Dinette Spice Cake with
Easy Penuche Icing

Cheese Soufflé

2 tbsp. butter	⅔ cup shredded sharp
2 tbsp. flour	cheese
¼ tsp. salt	2 egg yolks, well
pepper	beaten
cayenne pepper	2 egg whites
¼ tsp. mustard	¼ tsp. cream of
⅔ cup milk	tartar

Heat oven to 350° (mod.). Melt butter over low heat in heavy saucepan. Blend in flour and seasonings. Cook over low heat, stirring until mixture is smooth and bubbly. Remove from heat; stir in milk. Bring to boil, stirring constantly. Boil 1 min. Stir in cheese. Remove from heat; stir in egg yolks.

Beat egg whites and cream of tartar until stiff. Fold in the cheese mixture. Pour into ungreased 1-qt. baking dish. For a High Hat Soufflé, make groove 1″ from edge. Set baking dish in pan of hot water (1″ deep). Bake 50 to 55 min., until puffed and golden brown. Serve immediately with Seafood Sauce (below). *2 servings.*

Seafood Sauce

Carefully stir ½ to 1 cup cooked shrimp, lobster, crabmeat, salmon, or tuna pieces into 1 cup Medium White Sauce (p. 122).

The Cheese Soufflé is also delicious when served with Tomato Sauce (p. 76) or Mushroom Sauce (p. 122).

Buttered Broccoli

Wash ¾ lb. fresh broccoli. Trim tips of stems. Make 3 to 4 gashes through stems. Set upright in small pan. Cook, uncovered, in large amount of boiling salted water 10 to 15 min. Season with butter, salt, and pepper. *2 servings.*

Dinette Cake

1½ cups cake flour	⅓ cup soft
1 cup sugar	shortening
2 tsp. baking powder	⅔ cup milk
½ tsp. salt	1 tsp. flavoring
	1 egg

Heat oven to 350° (mod.). Measure flour by dipping method (p. 123) or by sifting. Stir the flour, sugar, baking powder, and salt together. Add shortening, milk, and flavoring. Beat 2 min. medium speed on mixer or 300 strokes by hand. Add egg. Beat 2 more min. Pour into greased and floured square pan, 9x9x1¾″. Bake 30 to 35 min., until toothpick stuck into center comes out clean.

Dinette Spice Cake

Follow directions for Dinette Cake (above)— except add 1 tsp. cinnamon, ½ tsp. nutmeg, and ¼ tsp. cloves with dry ingredients. Frost with Easy Penuche Icing (below).

Easy Penuche Icing

⅓ cup butter	3 tbsp. milk
⅔ cup brown sugar	1 to 1½ cups sifted
(packed)	confectioners' sugar

Melt butter in saucepan. Stir in brown sugar. Boil and stir over low heat 2 min. Stir in milk. Bring to boil, stirring constantly. Cool to lukewarm (120°). Gradually stir in confectioners' sugar. Place pan in ice water and stir until thick enough to spread. *For 9″ square cake.*

The Table Setting

For an informal dinner, use either a tablecloth or place mats, which may be of linen, cotton, straw, or plastic. A silence cloth or pad should be laid beneath the tablecloth (which should have a center crease only, running the length of the table). Colored linens or place mats with matching or harmonizing napkins are attractive, particularly if the glassware is colorless. The centerpiece should enhance the table but should be low enough not to obstruct the view of the diners. Place it either formally in the center or at an unused end of the table. Candlelight lends a festive air to dinner; white or ivory candles are best.

Allow 20 to 24 inches for each guest, measuring from center to center of place settings. Napkins, folded in squares or rectangles, are placed with open corner at the lower right, either in the center of each cover or to the left of the forks.

Place silver 1″ from table edge in a straight line with no more than three pieces on either side of the plate. Silver is used from the outside in on each side: on the left, first the dinner fork, then the salad fork, and dessert fork (all with prongs up); on the right, first the soup or bouillon spoon, then the teaspoon, and closest to the center, the knife with sharp blade toward the plate. Cocktail forks may be placed on the appetizer plate or at the extreme right. The water glass or goblet is placed directly above the point of the knife, cups and saucers at right of spoons with handles turned to right. Salad plates are set to the left of forks.

The salt and pepper, cream and sugar for coffee, and dessert silver may be on an informal table from the beginning of the meal, but all silver service pieces incidental to the serving of the main course are removed before the dessert.

Bread and butter plates may be used for an informal dinner. If used, the butter knife is placed horizontally across the top of each plate. Coffee may be served throughout the meal for those who wish it. After-dinner coffee is served either at the table with dessert or in the living room in demitasse cups with a short coffee spoon on each saucer.

Table Service

The host may carve and serve at the table, or plates may be filled in the kitchen and placed at each setting. Many hostesses use a tea wagon or cart on wheels to simplify service. It holds the salad, condiments, and dessert, which the hostess can serve gracefully from her left. The table may be cleared without her leaving her place; guests pass their used plates to her, she stacks them unobtrusively on the lower shelf of the cart and serves dessert from the upper tray. This permits her to remain with her guests throughout the meal, leaving only once in order to bring in coffee.

Dinner or luncheon forks may be used for salad and for dessert; dessert spoons may double for soup spoons and teaspoons may be used in place of round-bowled bouillon spoons with a clear soup. If desired, dessert silver—spoon or fork or both—may be brought in on the dessert plate, as at a formal dinner. Fruit knives are put on the table only as the fruit is served.

Relishes, pickles, and jellies that accompany the meat are placed on the dinner plate. Jams, jellies, olives, celery, and radishes, as well as crackers, are placed on the butter plate, if it is used.

Finger bowls may be used even at informal dinners and are a pleasant service, especially useful if food served is to be eaten with the fingers. The finger bowl is set on a thin doily and served on the dessert plate with the dessert silver. Both bowl and doily are removed by each guest and placed above and to the left of the place setting. The silver is placed at either side of the plate.

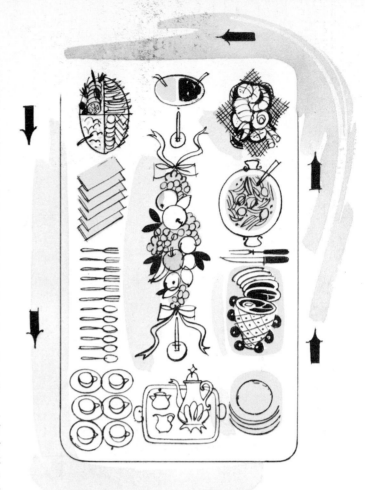

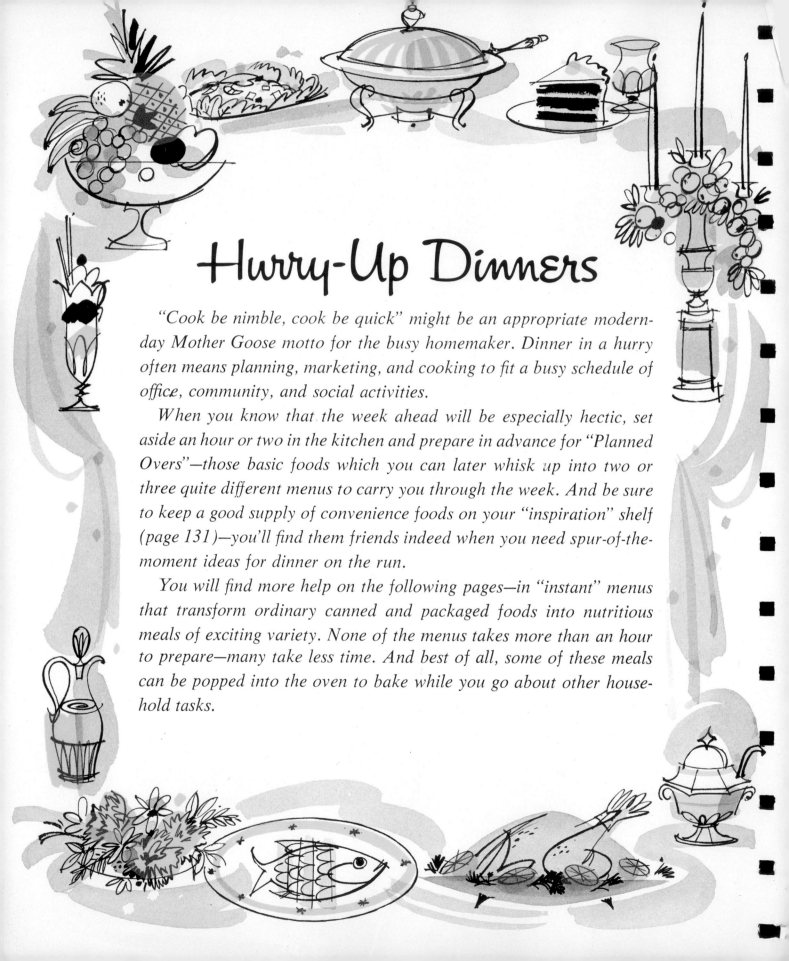

Hurry-Up Dinners

"Cook be nimble, cook be quick" might be an appropriate modern-day Mother Goose motto for the busy homemaker. Dinner in a hurry often means planning, marketing, and cooking to fit a busy schedule of office, community, and social activities.

When you know that the week ahead will be especially hectic, set aside an hour or two in the kitchen and prepare in advance for "Planned Overs"—those basic foods which you can later whisk up into two or three quite different menus to carry you through the week. And be sure to keep a good supply of convenience foods on your "inspiration" shelf (page 131)—you'll find them friends indeed when you need spur-of-the-moment ideas for dinner on the run.

You will find more help on the following pages—in "instant" menus that transform ordinary canned and packaged foods into nutritious meals of exciting variety. None of the menus takes more than an hour to prepare—many take less time. And best of all, some of these meals can be popped into the oven to bake while you go about other household tasks.

*Crispy Browned Hash
Lemon-buttered Broccoli
Lettuce-Raw Mushroom-Radish Salad
Hot Buttered Rye Bread
Orange Fluff
on Warm Gingerbread (p. 10)*

Crispy Browned Hash

You can use chopped cooked veal, lamb, ham, chicken, or turkey in place of beef when making hash.

1 cup chopped cooked beef	1 tbsp. minced parsley
1 cup chopped cooked potatoes	salt and pepper to taste
1 onion, minced	½ cup milk

Mix all ingredients except milk. Place a little fat in a hot heavy skillet over medium heat. When fat is very hot, spread hash evenly in skillet. The pan should be hot enough to brown the bottom of the hash quickly, 10 to 15 min. Add milk and mix. Cover and cook slowly until crisp, about 10 min. *2 servings.*

Red Flannel Hash

Make Crispy Brown Hash (above)—except use corned beef; substitute chopped beets for half of potatoes.

Lemon-buttered Broccoli

Cook 1 pkg. (10 oz.) frozen broccoli as directed on pkg. (or prepare fresh broccoli as directed on p. 62). Serve with Lemon Butter (p. 113). *2 servings.*

Lettuce-Raw Mushroom-Radish Salad

Toss torn lettuce, thinly sliced raw mushrooms, and sliced radishes with Oil-and-Vinegar Dressing (p. 59).

HOW TO PREPARE RAW MUSHROOMS

Wash mushrooms quickly in cold water; drain thoroughly—do not soak. If stem is discolored, cut off a thin slice. Always keep fresh mushrooms refrigerated; use within two or three days.

Hot Buttered Rye Bread

Heat oven to 400° (mod. hot). Spread slices of rye bread with generous amount of softened butter. Arrange bread on baking sheet. Heat about 10 min., until piping hot.

Orange Fluff

Also known as Russian Sauce.

3 or 4 egg yolks or 2 whole eggs	1 tbsp. grated orange rind
½ cup sugar	1 cup whipping cream, whipped stiff
⅓ to ½ cup orange juice (1 orange)	

Mix egg yolks, sugar, and orange juice in top of double boiler. Cook over hot water, stirring constantly, until it thickens (about 15 min.). Stir in orange rind. Cool. Fold in whipped cream. *Makes 4 cups.*

Leftover Fluff? Use as topping on white, sponge, or chiffon cake.

Chicken Caruso
Cucumber Sticks (p. 52)
Pear-Cranberry Relish Salad
Boston Cream Pie

Chicken Caruso

1 slice bacon, finely cut	1 cup cooked peas
¼ cup minced onion	⅛ tsp. each salt and pepper
¼ cup minced green pepper	1 cup hot drained boiled macaroni (½ cup uncooked)
1 cup cut-up cooked chicken	parsley
1 cup grated sharp Cheddar cheese (¼ lb.)	2 to 3 tbsp. toasted slivered almonds, if desired
2 tbsp. cut-up pimiento (2-oz. jar)	

In medium skillet, sauté bacon until lightly browned and crisp. Stir in onion and green pepper; cook until almost tender. Stir in chicken, cheese, pimiento, and peas; season with salt and pepper. Mix in cooked macaroni. Cover and keep warm over very low heat until ready to serve. Garnish with parsley sprigs; sprinkle with toasted almonds. *2 generous servings.*

Note: For best color, use cooked fresh or frozen peas.

Pear-Cranberry Relish Salad

For each salad, arrange a canned pear half on salad greens on an individual salad plate. Fill hollow of pear with Cranberry-Ginger Relish (below).

Cranberry-Ginger Relish

½ medium orange	½ tsp. ground ginger or 1 tbsp. finely chopped crystallized ginger
¾ cup plus 2 tbsp. whole cranberry sauce	
¼ cup white raisins	

Put orange (including rind and pulp) through food grinder or chop with knife. Mix in small bowl with remaining ingredients. Place in refrigerator several hours to blend flavors. *Makes 1 cup.*

Boston Cream Pie

Prepare 1 pkg. (about 3½ oz.) vanilla pudding and pie filling as directed on pkg. Cool and refrigerate. Prepare Velvet Crumb Cake in round layer pan, 9x1½″, as directed on buttermilk baking mix pkg. Remove cake from pan; cool. Split cake horizontally to make 2 layers. Fill layers with half of pudding, reserving remainder for future use. Spread top of cake with Thin Chocolate Icing (below). To serve, cut into pie-shaped wedges. Refrigerate any remaining cake. *Makes 12 servings.*

Thin Chocolate Icing: Melt 1 sq. unsweetened chocolate (1 oz.) and 1 tsp. butter together over hot water. Remove from heat. Blend in 1 cup confectioners' sugar and 2 tbsp. boiling water. Beat only until smooth but not stiff.

HURRY-UP DINNERS **69**

*Salmon Loaf
Baked "French Fried" Potatoes (p. 59)
Baby Green Limas (p. 96)
Fruit Salad with Whipped Topping*

*Minute or Cube Steaks
Fried Tomato Halves with Cream
Mashed Potatoes (p. 36)
Cracked Wheat Toast
Lime or Orange Parfait
Ginger Drop Cookies*

Salmon Loaf

1 egg
2 cups pink or red salmon, boned and flaked (skin discarded)
liquid from salmon plus milk to make ¾ cup (or use ¾ cup milk)

1½ cups coarse cracker crumbs
1 tbsp. lemon juice
1 tsp. chopped onion
⅛ tsp. each salt and pepper

Heat oven to 350° (mod.). Grease one half of a 9x5x3" loaf pan. Blend egg into flaked salmon. Stir in remaining ingredients. Spoon lightly into greased half of pan. Pat into loaf shape. Bake 45 min., until top is golden and crisp. Serve garnished with lemon wedges and parsley sprigs. Pass Egg Sauce, if desired. *4 servings.*

Egg Sauce

Prepare ½ cup Thin White Sauce (p. 122). Carefully stir in 1 diced hard-cooked egg. Season.

Whipped Topping

This is a low cost, low calorie topping for salads and simple desserts.

Place ¼ cup ice water in bowl and add ¼ cup dry skim milk powder slowly. Beat until stiff, about 10 min. Add ¼ cup sugar and 1 tbsp. lemon juice. Chill before serving. Whip again if topping separates. *Makes 1¼ cups.*

FRUIT SALAD FOR DESSERT

In summer, serve watermelon or cantaloupe balls, fresh pineapple wedges, or fresh peach slices. In winter, serve banana slices, canned apricot halves, or canned Bing cherries.

Minute or Cube Steaks

These steaks are inexpensive cuts of beef, ¼ to ½" thick, scored or cubed by a special machine that cuts the fibers, making the meat more tender.

Dip steaks in flour, shaking off any surplus. Place in sizzling hot skillet in just enough butter to keep meat from sticking. Pan-fry on one side 2 to 6 min., or until browned as you prefer. Turn, and pan-fry on other side 2 to 6 min. Remove to hot platter, sprinkle with salt and pepper; spread with softened butter. Serve immediately.

Fried Tomato Halves with Cream

Peel tomatoes; cut crosswise through center to make 2 thick slices. Sprinkle with salt, pepper, and sweet basil. Sauté in small amount of butter, turning to brown well on both sides. When done, remove to steak platter. Immediately pour cream into the hot skillet and let bubble over low heat until brown. Pour over tomatoes on platter or pass in separate bowl. Serve at once.

TIME–SAVER
Use instant mashed potato puffs and follow pkg. directions for preparing 2 servings.

Lime or Orange Parfait

Place alternate layers of lime or orange ice or sherbet and vanilla ice cream in chilled parfait glasses or sherbet cups.

Ginger Drop Cookies

Add ½ cup lukewarm water to 1 pkg. (14.5 oz.) gingerbread mix. Blend until smooth. Chill. Drop dough by teaspoonfuls onto lightly greased baking sheet. Bake in 375° (quick mod.) oven 10 to 12 min. *Makes 3 doz. cookies.*

Broiled Lamb Chops
Potatoes Anna   Minted Peas
Lettuce with
Thousand Island Dressing
Brown 'N Serve Cloverleaf Rolls
Frosty Lime Fruit Dessert

Broiled Lamb Chops

Allow ½ to ¾ lb. chops for each serving. Set oven regulator at 550° or "broil." Place chops on rack in broiler pan, having top surface of meat about 2″ from heat. Broil until top sides are brown (see below); season broiled side with salt and pepper. Turn chops. Brown other side; season with salt and pepper. Turn only once! Serve immediately.

	Medium	Well Done
Rib or Loin (1″ thick)	6 min. each side	7 min. each side
(1½″ thick)	9 min. each side	11 min. each side
Shoulder (1″ thick)		8 min. each side

Potatoes Anna

Melt 2 tbsp. butter in heavy skillet. Arrange thinly sliced or grated raw potatoes (about 2 medium) in 2 or 3 layers. Sprinkle each layer with salt and pepper; dot generously with butter. Cover; steam 15 min. Uncover; continue cooking until tender and crispy brown on the bottom. Invert on hot serving plate. *2 servings.*

Minted Peas

Add minced fresh mint to new peas while cooking; see recipe for Buttered Green Peas (p. 6). Or just before serving, add a tbsp. or two of green mint jelly to the cooked peas with the salt and pepper. Omit butter.

Thousand Island Dressing

Mix with ½ cup mayonnaise: 1 tbsp. chili sauce; 1 tbsp. chopped stuffed olives; 1 tsp. minced chives; 1 hard-cooked egg, chopped; ¼ tsp. paprika; and additional salt and pepper to taste. *Makes ¾ cup.*

Frosty Lime Fruit Dessert

Pour ⅓ cup thawed undiluted frozen limeade concentrate over 1½ cups fresh fruit, such as watermelon and cantaloupe balls, pineapple wedges, peach slices, banana slices. Let stand, covered, for a couple of hours in refrigerator. Spoon into chilled sherbet dishes. Top with sprigs of mint. *2 servings.*

Note: Dilute remaining limeade for use as a beverage.

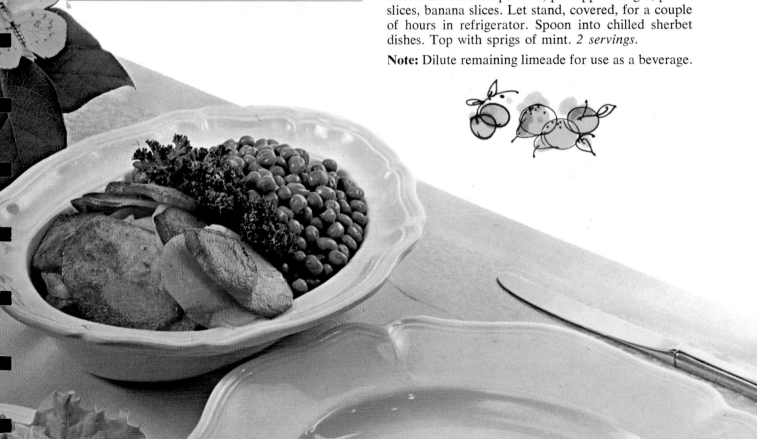

*Vegetable Cocktail
Chicken à la King over Toast Points
Buttered Asparagus
Pineapple and Cranberry Slices
Chocolate-covered Cherry Cookies*

Vegetable Cocktail

Blend 2 parts tomato juice and 1 part sauerkraut juice; chill. Or chill canned vegetable-juice cocktail.

Chicken à la King

⅓ cup (2-oz. can) mushrooms, drained
¼ cup chopped green pepper
¼ cup butter
¼ cup all-purpose flour
½ tsp. salt
⅛ tsp. pepper
1 cup chicken broth
1 cup milk or cream
1 cup diced cooked chicken
¼ cup chopped pimiento

Sauté mushrooms and green pepper in butter. Blend in flour and seasonings. Cook over low heat, stirring until mixture is smooth and bubbly. Remove from heat. Slowly stir in broth and milk. Bring to boil over low heat, stirring constantly. Boil 1 min. Add chicken and pimiento. Continue cooking until meat is heated through. Serve half (2 servings) of hot mixture over toast points, biscuits, or chow mein noodles. Refrigerate remaining half for use in Quick Trick Chicken and Rice (p. 73).

Quick Chicken à la King

Heat 1 can (10½ oz.) cream of mushroom soup. Stir in 1 can (5 oz.) boned chicken; 1 jar (2 oz.) pimientos, drained and cut up; and ½ cup cut-up celery, raw or cooked. Heat. Season with salt and pepper to taste. *2 servings.*

Buttered Asparagus

Select 1 lb. fresh asparagus. Break off stalks as far down as they snap easily. Remove scales along stems; wash well; leave whole. Tie whole stalks in bunches with string and stand upright in narrow deep pan or coffeepot. Cook, covered, in 1″ boiling salted water 10 to 20 min., until tender crisp. Catch string with fork when lifting asparagus out of pan to keep stalks whole. Season with salt and pepper. Pour melted butter over top. *2 servings.*

Pineapple and Cranberry Slices

For each serving, arrange a pineapple ring and jellied cranberry slice on salad greens. Top with favorite fruit dressing.

Chocolate-covered Cherry Cookies

½ cup soft butter
¾ cup sifted confectioners' sugar
1 tbsp. vanilla
1 sq. unsweetened chocolate (1 oz.), melted
1½ cups all-purpose flour
⅛ tsp. salt
20 to 25 maraschino cherries, well drained
Chocolate Icing (below)

Heat oven to 350° (mod.). Mix butter, sugar, vanilla, and chocolate thoroughly. Measure flour by dipping method (p. 123) or by sifting. Blend in flour and salt. If dry, add 1 to 2 tbsp. cream. Wrap level tablespoonful of dough around well-drained maraschino cherry. Place 1″ apart on ungreased baking sheet. Bake 12 to 15 min. Cool. Dip tops of cookies in Icing. Decorate, if desired, with shredded coconut, chopped nuts, or nut halves. *Makes 20 to 25 cookies.*

Chocolate Icing: Mix 1 cup sifted confectioners' sugar, ¼ cup cream, 1 tsp. vanilla, and 1 sq. unsweetened chocolate (1 oz.), melted.

Quick Trick Chicken and Rice
Tomatoes Vinaigrette
Broiled Zucchini
Peach Shortcake

Quick Trick Chicken and Rice

Place half of Chicken à la King (p. 72) and 1 cup cooked rice over low heat in saucepan or skillet. Stir in 2 tbsp. milk, cream, or chicken broth. Cover; heat through. If desired, place on individual serving dishes. Sprinkle 1 tbsp. toasted slivered almonds over each serving. *2 servings.*

Tomatoes Vinaigrette

A wonderful do-ahead salad.

Place 4 thick tomato slices or 2 whole small tomatoes, peeled, in small flat-bottomed dish. Spoon over tomatoes a mixture of: ½ cup olive oil, 2½ tbsp. wine vinegar, 1 tsp. oregano, ½ tsp. salt, 1 clove garlic (pressed or minced), ¼ tsp. pepper, and ¼ tsp. dry mustard. Cover. Refrigerate 2 to 3 hr. or overnight, spooning dressing over occasionally. At serving time, drain off some of the dressing and sprinkle tomatoes with minced onion and parsley. Serve on greens on salad plate. *2 servings.*

> *Peel tomatoes by placing in boiling water 1 min. Plunge into cold water. Skin will slip off easily.*

Broiled Zucchini

Select 2 tender, young small to medium zucchini squash; cut in half lengthwise. Cook in boiling salted water until just barely tender, about 5 min.; drain very well. Brush with melted butter; sprinkle with salt, pepper, paprika, and Parmesan cheese. Broil until cheese browns. *2 servings.*

Peach Shortcake

Peel and slice 2 peaches; sweeten with ⅓ cup sugar. Or thaw 1 pkg. (10 oz.) frozen peaches. Make 4 small Shortcakes (below). Split Shortcakes; fill and top with fruit. Top with whipped cream or coffee cream. *2 servings.*

Shortcakes

Heat oven to 450° (hot). Add ¼ cup milk, 1 tbsp. butter, melted, and 1 tbsp. sugar to 1 cup buttermilk baking mix. Mix thoroughly with fork. Keep dough soft; if too sticky, add more baking mix. Knead 10 times on floured surface. Pat or roll dough to ½″ thickness. (Shortcakes double in volume during baking.) Using a 3″ floured biscuit cutter, cut into 3 individual shortcakes. Bake on ungreased baking sheet about 10 min. *Makes 3 shortcakes.*

Leftover Shortcakes? Save for another meal. Serve with berries or another sweetened fruit and top with whipped cream.

> *For an interesting change, instead of dessert, pass a plate of chocolates or fudge with after-dinner coffee.*

*Shepherd's Pie
Slice of Lettuce
with favorite French Dressing
Whole Wheat Toast Triangles
Apple or Pineapple Crisp*

*Tuna-Broccoli Casserole
Hot French Bread
Grapefruit and Avocado Salad
Coconut Cream Pudding
Crisp Chocolate Wafers*

Shepherd's Pie

instant mashed potato puffs	1 cup beef or lamb gravy or 1 can (10¾ oz.) mushroom gravy
1½ cups diced cooked beef or lamb	
1 cup cooked vegetables	¼ tsp. salt

Heat oven to 350° (mod.). Prepare potatoes as directed on pkg. for 2 servings; set aside. Stir meat, vegetables, gravy, and salt together. Pour into 1-qt. baking dish. Mound potatoes in ring around edge of dish. Bake 30 min., or until potatoes brown slightly. *2 generous servings.*

Apple Crisp

2 cups sliced, pared, cored baking apples (about 2 medium)	¼ cup all-purpose flour
	¼ cup rolled oats
⅓ to ½ cup brown sugar (packed)	½ tsp. cinnamon
	½ tsp. nutmeg
	3 tbsp. soft butter

Heat oven to 350° (mod.). Place apples in greased 9x5x3″ loaf pan. Blend remaining ingredients until crumbly. Spread sugar-flour mixture over apples. Bake 30 to 35 min., until apples are tender and topping is golden brown. Serve warm with cream, whipped ice cream, or hard sauce. *2 generous servings.*

Pineapple Crisp

Make Apple Crisp (above)—except use 1 can (13½ oz.) pineapple tidbits, drained, in place of apples and reduce sugar to ¼ to ⅓ cup.

Tuna-Broccoli Casserole

1 pkg. (10 oz.) frozen broccoli	½ soup can milk
	½ cup crushed potato chips
1 can (7 oz.) tuna, flaked	
1 can (10½ oz.) cream of mushroom soup	

Heat oven to 450° (hot). Cook broccoli stalks about 3 min.; drain. Place in 1½-qt. baking dish. Cover with tuna. Mix soup and milk; pour over tuna. Sprinkle potato chips on top. Bake 15 min. *4 servings.*

Leftovers? You can make this casserole do for two meals. Keep refrigerated, and just reheat in 350° (mod.) oven.

Grapefruit and Avocado Salad

Using fresh avocado slices and canned or fresh grapefruit sections, arrange a fan of grapefruit slices and a fan of avocado slices on salad greens for each serving. Pass a favorite fruit dressing or Oil-and-Vinegar Dressing. (p. 59).

Coconut Cream Pudding

This pudding keeps well for a later meal.

1 cup (8 oz.) commercial sour cream	1 pkg. (3½ oz.) instant vanilla pudding
1 cup milk	1 cup toasted coconut

Combine sour cream and milk. Stir in pudding; blend, until mixture is smooth and slightly thickened. Stir in coconut, reserving a few tablespoonfuls for garnish. Chill 10 to 20 min., until pudding sets. *4 servings.*

*Ham and au Gratin Potatoes
Buttered Spinach
Apple and Grapefruit Salad
Coconut Tarts*

Ham and au Gratin Potatoes

Prepare 1 pkg. (5.5 oz.) au gratin potatoes as directed—except omit butter; stir 1½ cups cubed precooked ham into potatoes before baking them. Bake 35 to 40 min. *4 servings.*

Leftovers? Cover and reheat in mod. oven.

Planned-over au Gratin Potatoes with Ham

Prepare 1 pkg. (5.5 oz.) au gratin potatoes as directed. Serve for 2—about 2 servings will be left over.

Add 2 tbsp. water or milk to the 2 servings leftover au gratin potatoes in 1-qt. baking dish. Add ½ cup cubed ham. Cover and bake in 375° (quick mod.) oven 15 to 20 min. *2 servings.*

Apple and Grapefruit Salad

Arrange slices of unpared red apple and grapefruit sections (fresh or canned) on salad greens; pass a sweet dressing such as Limeade Dressing (p. 82).

Buttered Spinach

Buy about 1 lb. fresh spinach. Cut off any root ends and damaged leaves. Wash thoroughly. Cook 5 to 15 min., using only the water that clings to the leaves after washing. To preserve color, cook uncovered first 5 min. Serve with butter, salt, and pepper. *2 servings.*

To save time, prepare 1 pkg. (10 oz.) frozen leaf or chopped spinach as directed on pkg., or heat 1 can (8 oz.) spinach just to boiling.

Coconut Tarts

few drops of red and yellow food coloring	¼ cup flaked coconut 1 stick or ½ packet pie crust mix

Heat oven to 450° (very hot). Add food coloring to coconut to tint orange. Prepare pastry for One-crust Pie as directed on pkg.—except just before removing dough from bowl, work in coconut.

Divide dough into 8 equal portions and roll into 4″ rounds or 4″ squares. Pastry pieces may be fitted into individual pie pans or tart pans *or* they may be fitted over backs of muffin cups or small custard cups, making pleats so pastry will fit close. Prick with fork and place on baking sheets. Bake 8 to 10 min. (Watch closely as coconut will brown quickly when pastry is rolled thin.) When cool, remove from pans. Fill 2 tart shells with vanilla pudding for immediate serving. *8 tart shells.*

Leftover Tarts? Wrap unfilled tart shells in waxed paper and save for later use. Fill with ice cream, pudding, or diced fresh fruit.

*Puffy Omelet
with Tomato or Cahuenga Sauce
Crisp Bacon   Toasted English Muffins
Sliced Peaches with Orange Juice
Brown Sugar Drops*

Puffy Omelet

3 eggs, separated	1½ tbsp. butter
3 tbsp. milk or cream	your choice of sauce
salt and pepper	

Beat egg whites until stiff; beat egg yolks until thick and lemon-colored. Beat in milk or cream; add salt and pepper. Fold the beaten egg yolks into the beaten egg whites. Pour into sizzling butter in 8″ skillet. Turn heat to low. Cook slowly until light brown underneath, about 10 min. Bubbles will still appear through uncooked puffy top and mixture will look moist.

Meanwhile, heat oven to 350° (mod.). Place omelet in oven; bake 10 to 15 min., or until light brown on top and no imprint remains when touched lightly. Make ½″-deep crease across omelet. Slip pancake turner under, tip skillet to loosen omelet and fold in half without breaking. Roll omelet top-side-down onto hot platter. Surround with sauce. Serve immediately. *2 servings.*

BE PENNYWISE

Select canned goods economically. For example, you'll want top-quality peas to serve buttered for dinner but third-quality peas will make a delicious soup.

Tomato Sauce

Also delicious over veal cutlet or broiled hamburgers.

2 tbsp. chopped onion	1 can (8 oz.) tomato sauce
2 tbsp. chopped green pepper	salt and pepper to taste
1 tbsp. butter, melted	

Sauté onion and green pepper in butter until onion is transparent. Add sauce and seasonings; heat through. *Makes 1¼ cups.*

Cahuenga Sauce

Colorful, excitingly flavored.

¾ cup commercial sour cream	1 large tomato peeled and diced (don't use juice)
½ tsp. salt	
¼ tsp. dill seeds	1 small avocado, peeled and diced

Heat sour cream. Blend in salt and dill. Gently stir in drained diced tomato. Heat 1 min. Gently mix in diced avocado. *Makes about 1½ cups.*

Brown Sugar Drops

½ cup shortening (part butter or margarine)	¼ cup buttermilk or water
1 cup brown sugar (packed)	1¾ cups all-purpose flour
1 egg	½ tsp. soda
	½ tsp. salt
	½ cup chopped nuts

Mix shortening, brown sugar, and egg thoroughly. Stir in milk. Measure flour by dipping method (p. 123) or by sifting. Blend flour, soda, salt, and nuts; stir in. Chill at least 1 hr.

Heat oven to 400° (mod. hot). Drop rounded teaspoonfuls of dough 2″ apart on greased baking sheet. Bake 8 to 10 min., or until almost no imprint remains when touched lightly. *Makes 3 doz. 2½″ cookies.*

Date Brown Sugar Drops

Make Brown Sugar Drops (above)—except add ½ cup cut-up dates.

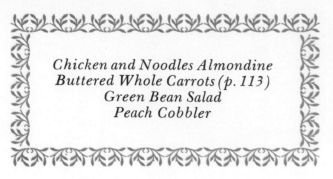

*Chicken and Noodles Almondine
Buttered Whole Carrots (p. 113)
Green Bean Salad
Peach Cobbler*

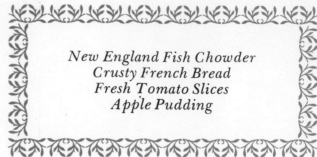

*New England Fish Chowder
Crusty French Bread
Fresh Tomato Slices
Apple Pudding*

Chicken and Noodles Almondine

Follow top-of-range method for 1 pkg. (6 oz.) noodles almondine, adding 1 cup cut-up cooked chicken and 1 can (4 oz.) mushroom stems and pieces, drained. *4 servings.*

Green Bean Salad

1 cup drained cooked or canned French-cut or cut green beans	1 tbsp. finely chopped onion
2 tbsp. French dressing	2 tbsp. grated Cheddar or Parmesan cheese

Marinate beans in dressing with onion several hours or overnight. Serve in lettuce cup. Sprinkle with cheese. *2 servings.*

Peach Cobbler

Canned apricot halves and cherries make wonderful cobblers, too.

1 can (8 oz.) sliced peaches	½ cup buttermilk baking mix
1½ tsp. cornstarch	2 tsp. sugar
1 tbsp. cold water	2 tbsp. milk
	1 tbsp. vegetable oil

Heat oven to 400° (mod. hot). Heat fruit with syrup. Blend in cornstarch dissolved in water. Bring to a boil; boil 1 min. Pour into 1-qt. baking dish. Stir baking mix and sugar together. Stir in milk and oil. Drop dough by spoonfuls over top of hot fruit. Bake 20 min. Serve hot with cream. *2 servings.*

New England Fish Chowder

1 lb. haddock or cod	½ cup chopped celery
1 cup boiling water	½ bay leaf, crumbled
¼ lb. salt pork, diced	1 tsp. salt
1 medium onion, sliced	¼ tsp. pepper
1 large potato, pared and diced	2 cups milk
	1 tbsp. butter

Simmer haddock, covered, in boiling water 15 min. Drain, reserving broth. Remove bones from fish. Sauté diced pork until crisp; remove and set aside. Sauté onion slices in pork drippings until golden brown. Add fish, potato, celery, bay leaf, salt, and pepper. Pour in fish broth plus enough additional boiling water to make 1½ cups liquid. Simmer covered 30 min. Add milk and butter; simmer 5 min. more. Serve chowder sprinkled with diced pork, if desired. *4 servings.*

Note: Fish chowders may be cooled, placed in plastic containers, and frozen for later use.

Apple Pudding

¾ cup fine zwieback crumbs or fine dry bread crumbs	⅛ tsp. salt
3 tbsp. butter	1½ tsp. lemon juice
1 cup applesauce	1 tsp. cinnamon
	⅛ tsp. nutmeg
	¼ cup whipping cream, whipped
	red jelly

Sauté crumbs in butter until evenly browned. Line greased 9x5x3″ loaf pan with half of crumbs. Mix applesauce, salt, lemon juice, and spices. Pour half over crumbs; cover with rest of crumbs, then pour on remaining applesauce mixture. Top with sweetened whipped cream. Chill several hours. Serve in squares decorated with bits of red jelly. *3 to 4 servings.*

Leftover Pudding? Refrigerate; serve another day.

Cheeseburger Broiled Dinner

½ lb. ground beef	pepper
½ cup fine dry bread or cracker crumbs	seasoned salt
¼ to ½ tsp. salt	1 medium tomato, halved, seasoned with salt and pepper
1 tbsp. dark steak sauce	2 very thin slices onion
½ cup tomato juice	2 thin slices sharp Cheddar cheese
1 can (8 oz.) whole potatoes, well drained	
butter	

Set oven to 550° (broil). Mix ground beef, crumbs, salt, steak sauce, and tomato juice. Lightly form into 2 thick patties; place on broiler pan rack. Arrange potatoes beside meat; dot with butter; sprinkle with pepper and seasoned salt. Broil about 4″ from heat until patties are browned (3 to 5 min.); turn. Again dot potatoes with butter; place tomato halves on rack beside potatoes. Broil 3 to 5 min. longer, until meat is browned. Cover each patty with an onion slice; top with a slice of cheese. Broil until cheese melts. *2 servings.*

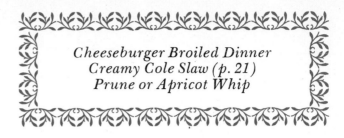

Cheeseburger Broiled Dinner
Creamy Cole Slaw (p. 21)
Prune or Apricot Whip

Prune or Apricot Whip

⅔ cup cut-up prunes or apricots (cooked, drained, pitted)	⅛ tsp. salt
	2 tsp. lemon juice
	2 tbsp. pecans, chopped
2 egg whites	
¼ cup sugar	

Beat fruit, egg whites, sugar, and salt at high speed on mixer until stiff peaks form, 4 to 5 min. Fold in lemon juice and pecans.

For Baked Whip: Pour into 1-qt. baking dish; set in pan of hot water (1″ deep) and bake in 350° (mod.) oven 30 to 35 min., or until puffed and a thin top coating has formed.

For Quick Whip: Spoon mixture directly into dessert dishes; chill.

Serve Whip with soft custard or sweetened whipped cream. *4 servings.*

Leftover Whip? Cover tightly and refrigerate; serve the next day.

Crabmeat Casserole
Corn Muffins　Buttered Peas (p. 6)
Lettuce and Tomato Salad
with Oil-and-Vinegar Dressing (p. 59)
Lemon Sherbet　Brownie Fudge Cake

Brownie Fudge Cake

A quick-to-make cake. Wonderful to have on hand.

Heat oven to 350°· (325° for glass pan). Grease a square pan, 9x9x1¾″. Empty 1 pkg. (15.5 oz.) regular size fudge brownie mix into small mixer bowl. Blend in ¼ cup water and 2 eggs. Beat 1 min. medium speed on mixer or 150 vigorous strokes by hand. Scrape sides and bottom of bowl often. Blend in another ¼ cup water. Beat 1 more min., scraping bowl often. Fold in ½ cup chopped nuts. Pour into prepared pan. Bake about 30 min. Frost with Quick Fudge Icing (below).

Crabmeat Casserole

½ cup milk	yolks of 3 hard-cooked eggs, mashed
¾ cup soft bread crumbs	¾ tsp. salt
1 can (7½ oz.) flaked cooked crabmeat	⅛ tsp. dry mustard dash of cayenne pepper
whites of 3 hard-cooked eggs, diced	3 tbsp. butter, melted buttered bread crumbs

Heat oven to 450° (hot). Mix milk and bread crumbs. Gently stir in crabmeat and diced egg whites. Blend in remaining ingredients. Place into buttered 9x5x3″ loaf pan or 1½-qt. baking dish. Sprinkle with buttered crumbs. Bake 15 min. *2 generous servings.*

Quick Fudge Icing

½ cup granulated sugar	dash of salt
2 tbsp. cocoa	¾ to 1 cup sifted confectioners' sugar
2 tbsp. butter	½ tsp. vanilla
¼ cup milk	
1 tbsp. light corn syrup	

Mix sugar and cocoa in saucepan. Stir in butter, milk, corn syrup, and salt; bring to full rolling boil. Boil vigorously 3 min., stirring occasionally. Cool. Beat in confectioners' sugar and vanilla.

Corn Muffins or Sticks

1 tbsp. sugar	⅔ cup buttermilk baking mix
1 egg	
¼ cup milk	⅓ cup corn meal

Heat oven to 450° (hot). Mix all ingredients; beat vigorously for 30 seconds. Fill well-greased muffin cups or corn stick pans ⅔ full. Bake 12 to 15 min. *Makes 6 muffins or 8 corn sticks.*

Leftover Muffins? Wrap in foil; reheat in oven.

Double-quick Corn Muffins

Measure contents of 1 pkg. (14 oz.) corn muffin mix; divide in half (about 1½ cups). Mix according to muffin directions except use 1 egg and ½ cup milk. *Makes 6 muffins.*

> *Chinese Beef and Rice*
> *Mandarin Orange-Apple Slice Salad*
> *Limeade or Lemonade Dressing*
> *Tapioca Cream*

Chinese Beef and Rice

⅔ cup rice	2 stalks celery,
2 tbsp. vegetable oil	chopped
1½ tsp. salt	1 green pepper,
1½ cups boiling water	chopped
1 bouillon cube	1½ cups diced
2 tsp. soy sauce	cooked beef
1 medium onion,	
chopped	

Cook rice in hot oil over medium heat until golden brown. Add salt, water, bouillon cube, and soy sauce. Cover; simmer 20 min. Add rest of ingredients. Cover tightly and simmer 10 min. more. (It may be necessary to add a little more water.) All water should be absorbed at end of cooking time. If not, remove cover and allow liquid to evaporate. *2 generous servings.*

Mandarin Orange-Apple Slice Salad

For each serving, alternate mandarin orange sections and unpared apple slices on salad greens. Top with Limeade or Lemonade Dressing (below).

Limeade or Lemonade Dressing

3 tbsp. undiluted	3 tbsp. honey
frozen concentrate	3 tbsp. vegetable oil
for limeade or	½ tsp. celery or
lemonade	poppy seeds

Combine all ingredients in small bowl. Beat with rotary beater until smooth. *Makes ½ cup.*

Tapioca Cream

1 egg yolk, slightly	⅛ tsp. salt
beaten	½ tsp. vanilla
1 cup milk	1 egg white
1 tbsp. sugar	2 tbsp. sugar
1 tbsp. quick-cooking	
tapioca	

Mix egg yolk, milk, 1 tbsp. sugar, tapioca, and salt in saucepan. Cook over low heat, stirring constantly, until mixture boils. Remove from heat; cool. Stir in vanilla. Beat egg white until frothy. Gradually beat in the 2 tbsp. sugar. Continue beating until stiff and glossy. Fold into mixture in saucepan. Spoon into dishes. Serve with cream. Chill. *2 servings.*

Chocolate Chip Tapioca Cream

Make Tapioca Cream (above)—except fold in ¼ cup semi-sweet chocolate pieces at the last.

Tomato Bouillon
Chicken or Seafood Salad
Buttered Peas with Pearl Onions
Hot Popovers
Pears Hélène

Tomato Bouillon

Combine equal parts tomato juice and bouillon (dilute canned bouillon or use cubes with boiling water). Serve hot.

Chicken Salad

For variety, use ¼ cup chopped salted almonds in place of bacon.

1 cup cut-up cooked chicken (large chunks)	salt and pepper to taste
½ cup cut-up celery (¼" pieces)	¼ cup mayonnaise
1½ tsp. lemon juice	1 or 2 hard-cooked eggs, cut up
	¼ cup finely broken crisp bacon

Toss chicken, celery, lemon juice, salt, and pepper together. Mix in mayonnaise. Carefully fold in eggs. Chill thoroughly. If desired, serve in tomato cups or on drained pineapple or avocado slices on salad greens. Sprinkle with the crisp bacon. *2 servings.*

Seafood Salad

Make Chicken Salad (above)—except use 1 cup flaked cooked seafood (crabmeat, shrimp, lobster, tuna, or salmon) in place of chicken.

Stewed Chicken

To avoid last-minute work, prepare your stewed chicken the day before. Cut it up the day you use it.

Place stewing chicken in kettle with tight-fitting cover. Add ½ cup water and ½ tsp. salt for each pound of ready-to-cook weight. For more flavor add 1 carrot, 1 small onion, 2 pieces of celery, and parsley. Bring to boiling; reduce heat and cook slowly until fork tender, 2 to 3 hr. Remove chicken; cool uncovered; then cover the chicken and broth and refrigerate. *A 3½- to 4-lb. stewing chicken yields 3 cups cooked chicken.*

Note: Cooked chicken is wonderful to have on hand. See the index for the many recipes that call for it.

Popovers

½ cup all-purpose flour	½ cup milk
¼ tsp. salt	1 egg

Heat oven to 450° (hot). Measure flour by dipping method (p. 123) or by sifting. Beat ingredients together with rotary beater just until smooth. Overbeating will reduce volume. Pour into well-greased deep muffin cups (¾ full) or oven-glass cups (½ full). Bake 25 min.; *lower oven temperature to 350° (mod.)* and bake 15 to 20 min. longer or until deep golden brown. If not baked long enough, they will collapse. Serve at once. *4 popovers.*

Pears Hélène

Place a drained, chilled canned pear half in each dessert dish. Top with vanilla ice cream. Cover with ready-made or Quick Chocolate Sauce (below).

Quick Chocolate Sauce

1 pkg. (6 oz.) semi-sweet chocolate pieces	⅛ tsp. salt
1 can (5½ oz.) evaporated milk	½ tsp. peppermint flavoring (not oil of peppermint), if desired

Melt chocolate over hot water. Beat in milk and salt. Blend in peppermint. Serve hot or cold. *Makes about 1½ cups.*

How to Meet a "Planned-Over"

When you follow the recipes and marketing tips in "Dinner for Two," you will rarely meet with a leftover. But when a favorite recipe or an economy purchase at the market leaves you with more than enough for a single meal, learn to look on the "leftover" as a blessing in disguise. A few vegetables, a cup of gravy, or left-over meat can be the beginning point for a second dinner, sometimes even more delicious than the first.

Here are a few ways in which to use leftovers:

- **Potatoes**—shape round patties and refrigerate or freeze between sheets of waxed paper. Brown lightly in butter and serve with meat.

- **Rice** —sauté with onion, then simmer in bouillon or broth with soy sauce to taste; add thin strips of leftover meat or poultry.

- **Eggs**—add yolks to custards, puddings, sauces.
  —use whites for meringues.
  —add whites or yolks to scrambled eggs.

- **Waffles or Pancakes**—refrigerate or freeze in layers between waxed paper. Reheat in single layer in 400° (mod. hot) oven for 5 min., turning once. Serve with creamed chicken or seafood for main course, or with ice cream and fruit for dessert.

• **Bread**—butter, cube, and toast for croutons to garnish soups and salads; crush with rolling pin and store covered in cool, dry place to use for crumbs in breading meats or making stuffing.

• **Fruits**—combine with fresh or canned fruits for fruit cocktails, salads, puddings, or refrigerator pies; or serve with nuts in sherbet dishes, well chilled, with thin custard sauce or whipped cream.

• **Cake**—break into pieces and mix with fruit and pudding, refrigerate and serve for dessert with whipped cream or fruit.

• **Vegetables**—serve hot in soups or casseroles.
—marinate, chill, and serve in salads.

Go one step farther, and like many creative cooks, make a practice of "Planned Overs." Plan one cooking session to provide the basis for two or more excellent meals. With a view to having a free day later in the week, purposely buy and roast a larger-than-necessary cut of beef, pork, or veal or a whole ham or leg of lamb. Then plan a savory stew with dumplings, a flavorful meat pie, or a casserole to serve with hot biscuits, muffins, or cornbread for a second dinner. Or stew a whole chicken, planning to build a second meal around chicken à la king, made from the cooked chicken meat.

You will find that "Planned Overs" save you both money and time in the kitchen; for the price of one cooking session, you get a work-free second dinner, and the pleasant feeling of security you have when you know that dinner is waiting for you, already more than half prepared, in the refrigerator.

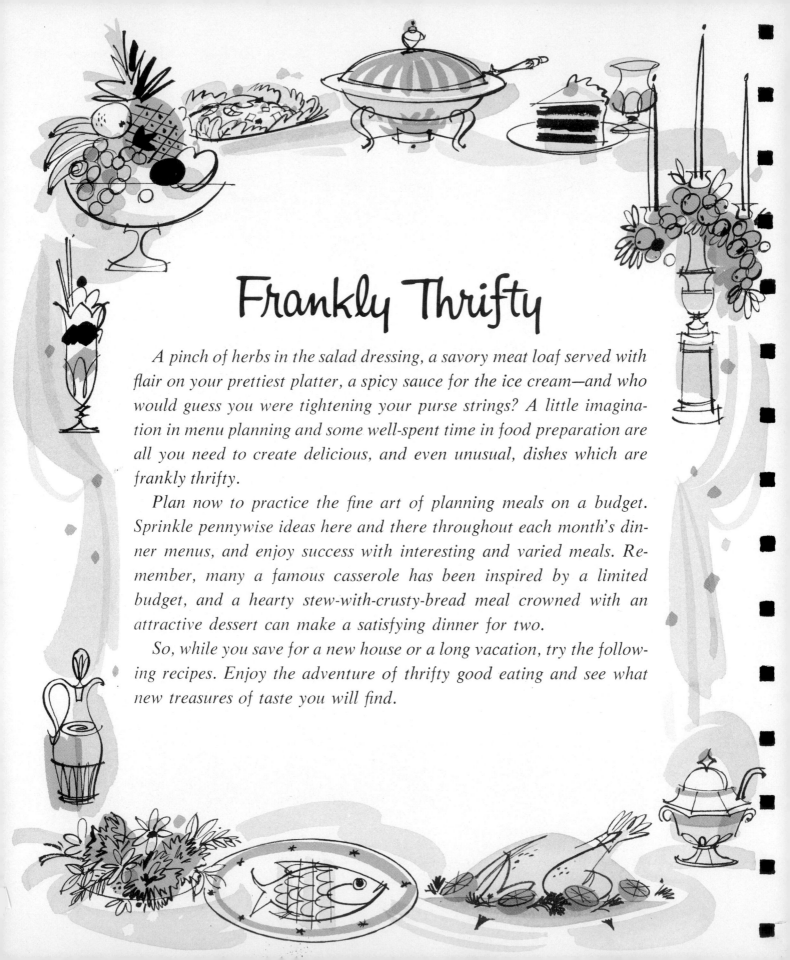

Frankly Thrifty

A pinch of herbs in the salad dressing, a savory meat loaf served with flair on your prettiest platter, a spicy sauce for the ice cream—and who would guess you were tightening your purse strings? A little imagination in menu planning and some well-spent time in food preparation are all you need to create delicious, and even unusual, dishes which are frankly thrifty.

Plan now to practice the fine art of planning meals on a budget. Sprinkle pennywise ideas here and there throughout each month's dinner menus, and enjoy success with interesting and varied meals. Remember, many a famous casserole has been inspired by a limited budget, and a hearty stew-with-crusty-bread meal crowned with an attractive dessert can make a satisfying dinner for two.

So, while you save for a new house or a long vacation, try the following recipes. Enjoy the adventure of thrifty good eating and see what new treasures of taste you will find.

Texas Hash
Celery Hearts   Dill Pickles
Heavenly Salad
Velvet Crumb
Upside-down Cake

Texas Hash

2 medium onions, sliced	1 cup cooked tomatoes
1 small green pepper, minced	¼ cup uncooked rice
1½ tbsp. fat	½ tsp. chili powder
½ lb. ground beef	1 tsp. salt
	dash of pepper

Heat oven to 350° (mod.). Sauté onions and green pepper in hot fat until yellow. Add ground beef and fry until mixture falls apart. Stir in remaining ingredients. Pour into greased 1-qt. baking dish. Cover and bake 1 hr., removing cover last 15 min. Serve hot. *2 generous servings.*

Heavenly Salad

Combine pineapple chunks or tidbits, sweet green grapes, and marshmallow cubes. Serve with 1-2-3 Fruit Dressing (right) or other sweet fruit salad dressing.

1-2-3 Fruit Dressing

1 egg, well beaten	juice and grated rind of 1 lemon, 1 lime, and 1 orange
1 cup sugar	

Combine all ingredients in saucepan. Cook over medium heat, stirring constantly, until boiling. Boil 1 min. Remove from heat; cool. Store in covered jar in refrigerator. *Makes 1½ cups.*

Velvet Crumb Upside-down Cake

2 tbsp. butter	Canned, fresh or cooked fruit (below)
¼ cup brown sugar (packed)	Velvet Crumb Cake batter

Heat oven to 350° (mod.). Melt butter over low heat in 8″ square pan, or 9″ round layer pan. Sprinkle with brown sugar. Arrange fruit over sugar mixture. Prepare Velvet Crumb Cake batter as directed on buttermilk baking mix pkg. Pour batter over fruit in pan. Bake 35 to 40 min., or until wooden pick inserted in center comes out clean. Invert at once onto serving plate; allow pan to remain over top a few minutes so sugar mixture will run down sides of cake. Serve warm or cold and, if desired, with whipped cream. *9 to 12 servings.*

For Pineapple Upside-down Cake: 1 can (9 oz.) sliced pineapple, drained. If desired, maraschino cherries and walnut or pecan halves can be added.

For Apricot Upside-down Cake: 1 can (1 lb.) apricot halves, drained, 1½ cups pitted halved apricots or 1½ cups stewed dried apricots. If desired, a pecan half can be placed in center of each apricot half.

Frankfurters with
Hot German Potato Salad
Crisp Vegetable Sticks (p. 10)
Caraway Rye Bread
Buttered Whole Green Beans (p. 59)
Singed Angel Wings

Frankfurters

Drop as many frankfurters as you will eat into boiling water. Reduce heat; simmer 5 to 8 min. Drain and serve immediately.

Hot German Potato Salad

2 medium potatoes	¾ tsp. salt
3 slices bacon	¼ tsp. celery seeds
⅓ cup chopped onion	dash of pepper
1 tbsp. flour	⅓ cup water
2 to 3 tsp. sugar	3 tbsp. vinegar

Boil potatoes in their jackets. Peel and slice thinly. Fry bacon slowly in skillet (p. 91); drain on absorbent paper; crumble. Sauté onion in bacon fat until golden brown. Blend in flour and seasonings. Cook over low heat, stirring until smooth and bubbly. Remove from heat. Stir in water and vinegar. Bring to boil, stirring constantly. Boil 1 min. Stir potatoes and crumbled bits of bacon in carefully. Remove from heat; cover and let stand until ready to serve. *2 generous servings.*

Singed Angel Wings

Glorified leftover angel food cake.

Brush cut sides of wedges of angel food cake with melted butter. Lightly brown both sides under broiler, about 1 min. per side. Spread with strawberry jam.

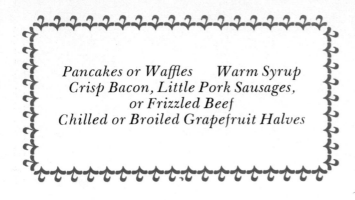

Pancakes or Waffles   Warm Syrup
Crisp Bacon, Little Pork Sausages,
or Frizzled Beef
Chilled or Broiled Grapefruit Halves

Pancakes

1 cup buttermilk baking mix	1 egg (small)
	¾ cup milk

Beat ingredients with rotary beater until smooth. Pour batter from pitcher onto hot griddle or lightly greased skillet. Turn pancakes when bubbles appear. *Makes 8 to 10 pancakes.*

Waffles

1 cup buttermilk baking mix	¾ cup milk
1 egg (small)	1 tbsp. vegetable oil or melted shortening

Beat ingredients with rotary beater until smooth. Pour batter from cup or pitcher onto center of hot waffle iron. Do not keep iron open longer than necessary. Bake until steaming stops. *Makes 1 large or 3 small waffles.*

To save time, delicious pancakes and waffles can be made from buttermilk pancake mix.

Griddle or waffle iron is right temperature for baking when a few drops of water sprinkled on it jump around.

Cheese and Bacon Waffles

To give your waffle supper a novel touch, try this variation.

Follow recipe for Waffles (above)—except stir in ¼ cup grated sharp cheese. After pouring batter onto hot waffle iron, lay short strips of crisp bacon across the batter. Bake. Serve with warm syrup.

Little Pork Sausages

Place links in skillet; add ¼" of water. Cover; simmer 5 min. Drain. Pan-fry until brown. Never prick. Or bake in 400° (mod. hot) oven 20 to 30 min.

Frizzled Beef

Lightly brown dried beef pieces in small amount of butter or fat. Keep heat low and stir frequently to prevent burning.

Three Ways to Cook Bacon

Pan-fried: In cold skillet over low heat, place overlapping slices just as they come from the pkg. As bacon slowly heats, separate slices so they lie flat on bottom of skillet. Spoon off excess fat as it accumulates. Turn to cook evenly. Cook 5 to 6 min., until crisp but not brittle. Drain bacon on absorbent paper. Keep warm.

Broiled: Place separated slices on broiling rack in pan 3" from heat. Turn once to brown evenly.

Baked: Heat oven to 400° (mod. hot). Place separated slices on rack in pan. Bake about 10 min., until crisp but not brittle. Do not turn.

Broiled Grapefruit Halves

Remove seeds and center from grapefruit halves. Cut around sections. Sprinkle with a bit of sugar (granulated, brown, or maple). Broil slowly 15 to 20 min., until heated. Add a little maraschino cherry juice or sherry flavoring. Serve hot.

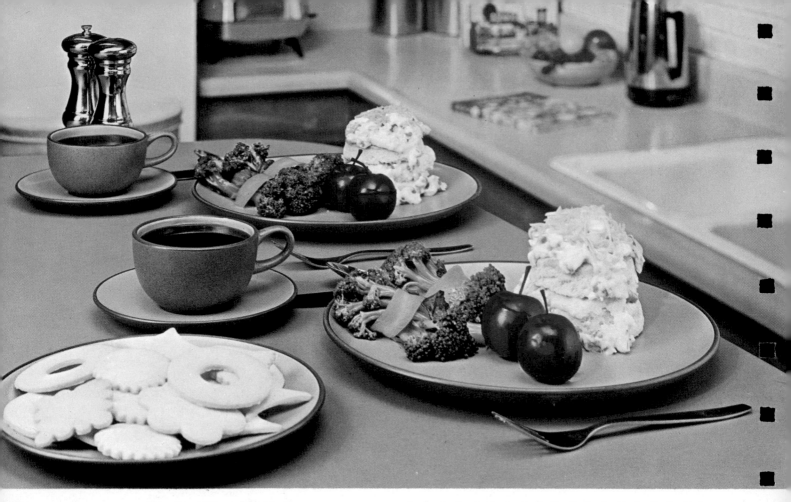

Glorified Egg Shortcake

Also delicious over chow mein noodles.

2 tbsp. butter	⅓ cup cooked or canned green peas
2 tbsp. flour	3 hard-cooked eggs, quartered
½ tsp. salt	Rolled Biscuits (p. 123)
⅛ tsp. pepper	2 to 3 tbsp. grated American or Cheddar cheese
1 cup milk	
2 tsp. chopped onions or chives	
1 tbsp. chopped pimiento, if desired	
⅓ cup thinly sliced celery	

Melt butter; blend in flour, salt, and pepper. Cook over low heat, stirring until mixture is smooth; remove from heat. Slowly stir in milk. Bring to a boil over direct heat, stirring constantly. Boil 1 min. Just before serving, stir in rest of ingredients except Biscuits and cheese. Bring mixture just to a boil. Serve over Biscuits. Sprinkle cheese over top. *2 generous servings.*

Glorified Egg Shortcake
Buttered Broccoli (p. 62)
Spiced Crabapples
Orange Delight
Mary's Sugar Cookies (p. 30)

Orange Delight

Place a scoop of orange sherbet or ice in each sherbet glass. Garnish with orange segments (white membrane removed) or mandarin orange sections. Pour orange juice over top.

Macaroni Beef Sauté
Green Beans   Anadama Bread (p. 24)
Onion-Cucumber Salad
Pineapple Sherbet
with Date Bar Drop Cookies

Date Bar Drop Cookies

Heat oven to 400° (mod. hot). Mix date filling from 1 pkg. (14 oz.) date bar mix and ¼ cup hot water. Add the crumbly mixture from pkg. and 1 egg; mix thoroughly. Drop rounded teaspoonfuls of dough about 2″ apart onto lightly greased baking sheet. Bake 8 to 10 min. Cool on wire rack. *Makes about 2½ doz. cookies.*

Macaroni Beef Sauté

½ lb. ground beef	1 can (12 oz.) tomato
½ cup uncooked elbow	juice (about 1⅔
macaroni (2 oz.)	cups)
¼ cup chopped onion	¾ tsp. salt
¼ cup chopped green	⅛ tsp. pepper
pepper	1 tsp. Worcestershire
½ clove garlic, minced	sauce
¼ cup vegetable oil	

Sauté beef, macaroni, onion, green pepper, and garlic in hot oil until macaroni turns slightly yellow. Drain off excess fat. Add tomato juice and seasonings; bring to boil. Cover and simmer 20 min. Uncover and simmer for several more min., or until sauce is reduced to desired consistency. *2 servings.*

Green Beans

Pour liquid from 1 can (8 oz.) green beans into small saucepan; boil down to half the amount. Add green beans; cover. Leave over heat several min., just long enough to heat through; drain. Season with salt and pepper. Serve sprinkled with grated Parmesan cheese. *2 servings.*

Onion-Cucumber Salad

½ cucumber	2 to 3 tsp. sugar
¼ medium onion	⅛ tsp. salt
¼ cup vinegar	dash of pepper
¼ cup water	

Pull tines of fork firmly down length of cucumber, repeating around cucumber; slice thinly. Thinly slice onion, separating rings. Combine remaining ingredients. Pour over vegetables; marinate at least 1 hr. Drain and arrange vegetables on salad greens. *2 servings.*

BE PENNYWISE

Stop, look, and save those leftovers! Meat or vegetable tidbits can reappear in a tossed salad, a soup, or a casserole. Cooky crumbs make an easy pie crust, while cake pieces make wonderful refrigerator desserts.

Meat Loaf
Baked (p. 25) or Scalloped (p. 18) Potatoes
Easy Creamed Spinach
Celery Sticks and Apple Wedges
Raspberry Cream

Easy Creamed Spinach

With sharp knife or frozen-food saw, cut 1 pkg. (10 oz.) frozen chopped spinach in half. (Return remaining half-pkg. to freezer for later use.) Partially thaw spinach and break apart. Make ½ cup Thick White Sauce (p. 122) in top of double boiler; add spinach and dash of nutmeg. Cover and cook over boiling water about 15 min., stirring occasionally. *2 servings.*

Meat Loaf

½ lb. ground beef or veal	1 egg, beaten
¼ lb. ground lean pork	2 tbsp. minced onion
1½ medium slices soft bread, torn in pieces, and ½ cup milk; or ½ cup dry bread crumbs and ⅔ cup milk	½ tsp. salt
	⅛ tsp. each pepper, dry mustard, celery salt, and garlic salt
	1½ tsp. Worcestershire sauce
	catsup

Heat oven to 350° (mod.). Mix all ingredients thoroughly. Shape into 2 loaves in shallow baking pan. Spread with catsup or your favorite bottled barbecue sauce. Bake 1 hr., until done. *4 servings.*

Note: Serve one loaf hot; serve the other cold for another dinner.

Raspberry Cream

1 pkg. (3 oz.) raspberry-flavored gelatin	1 pkg. (10 oz.) un-thawed frozen raspberries
1 cup boiling water	½ pt. vanilla ice cream, softened

Dissolve gelatin in water. Stir in the raspberries and ice cream. Refrigerate until set, about 20 min. Spoon into serving dishes. *4 servings.*

Note: Store any left over in the refrigerator.

Polish Sausages and Sauerkraut
Dumplings (p. 98) or Boiled Potatoes
Assorted Fresh Vegetable Relishes
Cherry Tower Pies

Cream of Corn Soup
Corned Beef Sandwiches
Crisp Relishes
Quickie French Tarts

Polish Sausages and Sauerkraut

1 can (1 lb.) sauerkraut
4 medium or 2 long Polish sausages
¼ tsp. caraway seeds
1½ tbsp. sugar
1½ tbsp. chopped onion
2 cups water
Dumplings (p. 98), if desired

Put all ingredients except dumplings into saucepan; simmer over low heat 1 hr. If desired, spoon batter for 2 large dumplings onto sauerkraut; cook uncovered over low heat 10 min.; cover and cook 10 min. more. *2 servings.*

Boiled Potatoes

Wash 2 medium potatoes; remove eyes. Pare thinly; leave whole. Cook, covered, in boiling salted water about 30 to 35 min., until tender. Drain; shake potatoes over low heat to dry. Serve with butter, salt, and pepper. *2 servings.*

Cherry Tower Pies

Using 2 Pastry Squares or Rounds (below) for each pie, spoon cherry filling from 1 can (1 lb. 4 oz.) cherry pie filling between and on top. Top with whipped cream or ice cream.

Pastry Squares or Rounds

Heat oven to 450° (very hot). Prepare pastry for One-crust Pie as directed on pie crust mix pkg. Roll out ⅛" thick on floured cloth-covered board. Cut into eight 3½" squares with sharp knife or pastry wheel or into large rounds with cooky cutter. Place on baking sheet. Prick well. Bake 8 to 10 min., until lightly browned. *Makes 8 squares or rounds.*

Leftover Squares or Rounds? Wrap in foil. Serve another day with filling of lemon, butterscotch, or chocolate pudding.

Cream of Corn Soup

½ tsp. finely chopped onion
1 tbsp. butter
1 to 1½ tbsp. flour
½ tsp. salt
dash of pepper
1 cup cream-style corn (8-oz. can)
2 cups milk

Sauté onion in butter. Blend in flour, salt, and pepper. Stir over medium heat until smooth and bubbly. Stir in corn. Bring to boil; boil 1 min., stirring constantly. Remove from heat. Gradually stir in milk. Heat to serving temperature. *2 generous servings.*

Quickie French Tarts

Spread two Short Pie Rounds (p. 103) with softened cream cheese. Pile fresh, frozen, or drained canned berries on cheese. Glaze with currant jelly heated with a little water. Serve immediately. *2 servings.*

Porcupines
Baby Green Limas
Festival Peach Salad
Chocolate Parfaits

Porcupines

½ lb. ground beef
¼ cup uncooked rice
¼ cup milk or water
2 tbsp. chopped onion
½ tsp. salt
¼ tsp. celery salt
⅛ tsp. garlic salt
dash of pepper

1 tbsp. shortening
  or drippings
1 can (8 oz.) tomato
  sauce
½ cup water
1½ tsp. Worcestershire
  sauce

Mix beef, rice, milk, onion, and seasonings. Form into 4 medium balls. Fry in melted shortening, turning frequently, until light brown (but not crusty) on all sides. Add tomato sauce, water, and Worcestershire sauce. Mix well. Cover; simmer 45 min. over low heat. Add a small amount of additional water if liquid cooks down too much. *2 servings*.

Baby Green Limas

You'll need about 1½ lb. Lima beans in shells. Snap pods open; remove beans. Or cut thin strip from inner edge of pod with knife; push beans out. Cook, covered, in ½ to 1″ boiling salted water 20 to 30 min. Season with butter, salt, and pepper. *2 servings*.

To save time, use 1 pkg. (10 oz.) frozen Lima beans. Cook as directed on pkg.

Festival Peach Salad

1 fresh peach or 2
  canned peach halves
¼ cup small curd
  cottage cheese
1 tbsp. toasted
  slivered almonds

1 tbsp. chopped
  maraschino cherries,
  well drained
1 tbsp. flaked coconut
lettuce leaves

Peel, halve, and pit fresh peach; sprinkle with lemon juice to prevent discoloration. Mix cottage cheese with almonds and cherries. Fill centers of peach halves with cottage cheese mixture; sprinkle with coconut. Serve on lettuce leaves. *2 servings*.

Chocolate Parfaits

Alternate layers of ice cream and Quick Chocolate Sauce (p. 85) in parfait glasses.

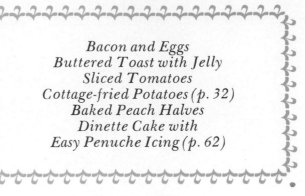

Bacon and Eggs
Buttered Toast with Jelly
Sliced Tomatoes
Cottage-fried Potatoes (p. 32)
Baked Peach Halves
Dinette Cake with
Easy Penuche Icing (p. 62)

Bacon and Eggs

Pan-fry bacon as directed on p. 91. Drain off excess fat, leaving a thin layer of bacon fat in skillet. With skillet moderately hot, break eggs, one at a time, into saucer; slip into skillet. Immediately reduce heat to low. Cook slowly, spooning fat over eggs until whites are set and a film forms over yolks (3 to 4 min.). Sprinkle with salt and pepper. Serve at once on warm plates.

Baked Peach Halves

Heat oven to 425° (hot). Place drained peach halves hollow-side-up in baking dish with a bit of butter in each. Sprinkle with nutmeg and stud with toasted slivered almonds. Pour a little fruit juice around peaches. Bake 12 min. Serve warm or cold.

BE PENNYWISE

Check recipes carefully. A recipe that looks thrifty may not be. Here's an example: ground beef recipes calling for sour cream or fresh mushrooms may be quite high in price, while a ground beef-rice-tomato combination would be low in price.

Old-fashioned Vegetable Soup

Homemade soup is wonderful to have on hand for hurried lunches or suppers.

1 beef soupbone with meat	1 can (1 lb.) tomatoes (2 cups)
1 to 2 tbsp. fat	3 sprigs parsley, finely cut
4 cups water	1 tbsp. salt
1 medium onion, chopped	½ bay leaf, crumbled
1 cup sliced carrots (2 or 3 medium)	3 peppercorns
1 cup cut-up celery and leaves (2 long stalks)	¼ tsp. marjoram
	¼ tsp. thyme

Cut meat off bone into small chunks. Brown in hot fat in large kettle. Add water and bone and simmer covered 1½ to 2 hr. Remove bone and skim fat from top of soup. Add vegetables, salt, bay leaf and peppercorns tied in cheesecloth bag, marjoram, and thyme; cook an additional 20 to 30 min., until vegetables are tender. Remove cheesecloth bag before serving. *6 to 8 servings.*

Note: Pour soup in plastic container and freeze. Always ready to heat and serve.

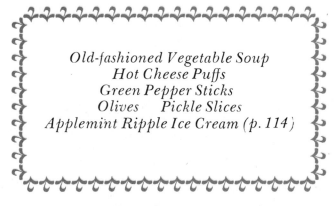

Old-fashioned Vegetable Soup
Hot Cheese Puffs
Green Pepper Sticks
Olives   Pickle Slices
Applemint Ripple Ice Cream (p. 114)

Hot Cheese Puffs

3 slices of bread	¼ tsp. paprika
2 egg whites	1 cup grated sharp Cheddar or Swiss cheese
½ tsp. baking powder	
¼ tsp. salt	

Cut each slice of bread into thirds or quarters. Toast bread on one side only under broiler. Beat egg whites until stiff. Fold in remaining ingredients; spread ¼" thick on untoasted side of bread slices. Broil until browned, about 5 min. *2 servings.*

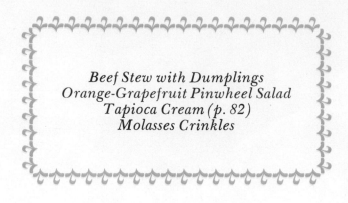

Beef Stew with Dumplings
Orange-Grapefruit Pinwheel Salad
Tapioca Cream (p. 82)
Molasses Crinkles

Beef Stew with Dumplings

1 lb. boneless beef chuck, cut in 1" cubes	1 small bay leaf, crumbled
2 cups water	1 tsp. salt
½ tsp. lemon juice	⅛ tsp. pepper
½ tsp. Worcestershire sauce	pinch of allspice
½ clove garlic, minced	½ tsp. sugar
½ medium onion, sliced	3 carrots, halved
	4 small onions
	1 to 2 potatoes, pared and quartered
	Dumplings (below)

Brown meat thoroughly on all sides in heavy saucepan. Add all ingredients except carrots, whole onions, potatoes, and Dumplings. Cover tightly. Cook 1 hr. 45 min. Add vegetables; cook 10 min. Add Dumplings; finish cooking stew with Dumplings. *4 servings.*

Note: If you wish to thicken broth, remove stew to hot platter. Slowly stir in ½ cup water and ¼ cup all-purpose flour which have been shaken in a jar. Bring to boil and boil for 1 min. Season and serve.

Dumplings

Mix 3 tbsp. milk with ½ cup buttermilk baking mix. Spoon batter lightly onto bubbling stew. Cook 10 min. uncovered and 10 min. covered. Remove. Top stew with Dumplings on warm plates.

Orange-Grapefruit Pinwheel Salad

Arrange orange and grapefruit sections alternately in pinwheel pattern on lettuce on each salad plate. Garnish center with sprig of deep green garnish (watercress, mint, parsley). Pass Ruby Red Dressing (p. 9).

Molasses Crinkles

¾ cup shortening	2 tsp. soda
1 cup brown sugar (packed)	¼ tsp. salt
1 egg	1 tsp. cinnamon
¼ cup molasses	1 tsp. ginger
2¼ cups all-purpose flour	½ tsp. cloves

Mix shortening, sugar, egg, and molasses thoroughly. Measure flour by dipping method (p. 123) or by sifting. Blend flour and rest of ingredients together. Stir into shortening mixture. Chill dough.

Heat oven to 375° (quick mod.). Roll dough into 1¼" balls. Dip tops in granulated sugar. Place sugared-side-up 3" apart on greased baking sheet. Sprinkle each cooky with 2 or 3 drops of water. Bake 10 to 12 min. *Makes 4 doz. cookies.*

BE PENNYWISE

But pennywise must never be nutrition-foolish. You must have the following foods every day:

Milk: *Two or more cups daily, directly or in other foods.*

Meat: *Two or more servings daily of meat, poultry, fish, or eggs.*

Vegetables and Fruit: *Four or more servings daily, including green or yellow vegetables and citrus fruits.*

Bread and Cereals: *Four or more servings daily from enriched or whole grains.*

Macaroni and Cheese

1 cup uncooked macaroni (4 oz.)	1 cup milk
4 oz. sharp cheese, cut up (1 cup)	½ tsp. salt dash of pepper paprika

Drop 4 oz. macaroni into 3 cups rapidly boiling salted water (2 tsp. salt). Bring back to rapid boil. Cook, stirring constantly, for 3 min. Cover with tight-fitting lid, remove from heat, and let stand 10 min. Rinse with hot water; drain.

Heat oven to 350° (mod.). Place alternating layers of macaroni, cheese, and milk in greased 1-qt. baking dish. Sprinkle with salt, pepper, and paprika. Bake 35 to 45 min., until golden brown on top. *4 servings.*

Leftover Macaroni and Cheese? Combine with ½ lb. cooked hamburger; heat and serve another time.

BE PENNYWISE
Use non-fat dry milk. Prepare a quart and keep it in the refrigerator to use in all your cooking, especially White Sauce (p. 122).

Macaroni and Cheese
Mexican Green Bean Salad
Seasoned Stewed Tomatoes
Crusty Bread
Fresh Fruit in Season

Mexican Green Bean Salad

Marinate 1 cup cooked French-cut green beans in 1 to 1½ tbsp. French dressing with 1 tbsp. minced onion about 2 hr. Add 1 to 1½ tbsp. grated American or Parmesan cheese. Garnish with red or white onion rings, if desired. *2 servings.*

Seasoned Stewed Tomatoes

An 8-oz. can is just right for two. Season with a little sugar, dash of salt and pepper, a little butter, and a bit of minced onion or chives.

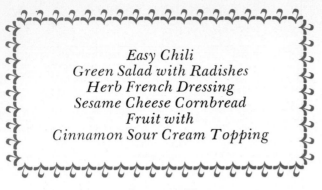

Easy Chili
Green Salad with Radishes
Herb French Dressing
Sesame Cheese Cornbread
Fruit with
Cinnamon Sour Cream Topping

Easy Chili

1⅓ cups Three-in-One Hamburger Mix (below)	½ to 1 cup tomato juice
1 can (15 oz.) kidney beans, including liquid	2 to 3 tsp. chili powder

Heat Hamburger Mix slowly in saucepan. Add remaining ingredients; heat. *2 generous servings.*

Three-in-One Hamburger Mix

½ cup chopped onion	1½ tsp. Worcestershire sauce
1 tbsp. butter	
2 lb. ground beef	1½ tsp. salt
⅔ cup catsup	1 tsp. vinegar
½ cup water	½ tsp. flavor enhancer (monosodium glutamate)
¼ cup chopped celery	
2 tbsp. lemon juice	
1 tbsp. brown sugar	¼ tsp. dry mustard

Sauté onion in butter. Add beef and brown lightly. Drain off excess fat. Add rest of ingredients; simmer covered for 30 min. Cool. *Makes 4 cups.*

Note: Use 1⅓ cups for Easy Chili (above). Freeze remaining mixture in two separate equal amounts (1⅓ cups each). Use one amount for Barbecued Hamburgers (below) and the other for Cheese-broiled Barbecue (right). Thaw before using.

Barbecued Hamburgers

Heat 1⅓ cups Three-in-One Hamburger Mix (above) slowly in skillet. Use as filling for hot buttered hamburger buns. *Makes enough for 4 buns.*

Cheese-broiled Barbecue

Heat 1⅓ cups Three-in-One Hamburger Mix (left). Butter split English muffins lightly; toast in oven or under broiler. Top each half with some of beef mixture and a slice of process American cheese. Place under broiler until cheese bubbles and is lightly browned. *Makes enough for 8 English muffin halves.*

Green Salad with Radishes

Tear 2 cups crisp, cold salad greens into bite-size pieces. Toss with ½ cup sliced radishes and Herb French Dressing (below). *2 servings.*

Herb French Dressing

¼ cup olive oil or vegetable oil	⅛ tsp. dry mustard
	⅛ tsp. paprika
1 tbsp. vinegar	1 tsp. minced parsley
1 tbsp. lemon juice	dash of thyme
¼ tsp. salt	¼ tsp. oregano

Shake ingredients together in tightly covered jar. *Makes ⅓ cup.*

Sesame Cheese Cornbread

Heat oven to 400° (mod. hot). Blend 1 egg and 1 cup milk in bowl. Add 1 pkg. (14 oz.) corn muffin mix, ½ tsp. salt, and 1 cup grated sharp Cheddar cheese. Stir with fork until blended; batter will be slightly lumpy. Pour into greased square pan, 8x8x2″ or 9x9x1¾″. Sprinkle with 3 tbsp. toasted sesame seeds. Bake 20 to 25 min. *9 servings.*

Leftover Cornbread? Wrap in foil and reheat in moderate oven.

Cinnamon Sour Cream Topping

¼ cup commercial sour cream	⅛ tsp. cinnamon dash of nutmeg
2 tsp. sugar	

Blend all ingredients together. Serve over fresh, canned, or frozen fruit. Garnish with toasted coconut or toasted chopped almonds. *Makes ¼ cup.*

Barbecued Lamb Riblets
Hot Buttered Noodles
Panned Cabbage
Pineapple-Cheese Salad
Spicy Raisin Cupcakes

Barbecued Lamb Riblets

Have meat dealer cut a 1½- to 2-lb. lamb breast in half, cutting across bones. Heat oven to 325° (slow mod.). Cut lamb breast into serving pieces of one, two, or three bones per piece. Place in large baking pan. Sprinkle with salt and pepper. Bake 1½ hr. uncovered. Pour off excess fat. Cover with Barbecue Sauce (below); bake covered 30 to 45 min. Garnish with lemon slices or wedges. *2 servings.*

Barbecue Sauce

½ cup catsup	½ tsp. salt
¼ cup vinegar	½ medium onion,
¼ cup water	minced
1 tbsp. Worcestershire sauce	

Mix ingredients. Pour over riblets. *Makes 1 cup.*

Hot Buttered Noodles

Cook 2 to 3 oz. noodles (about 1 cup) in 1½ qt. boiling salted water (1½ tsp. salt). Drain. Add 2 tbsp. butter and toss gently. *2 servings.*

Panned Cabbage

1 tbsp. fat	1½ cups shredded
½ tsp. beef extract	cabbage
dash of salt	

Blend and heat fat, beef extract, and salt in skillet. Add cabbage. Cover tightly and cook over very low heat until tender, about 10 min. *2 servings.*

Pineapple-Cheese Salad

For each serving, place a pineapple ring on salad greens. Top with dab of mayonnaise and grated Cheddar cheese.

Spicy Raisin Cupcakes

Prepare these ahead of time.

1 cup raisins	½ tsp. nutmeg
1 cup water	¼ cup shortening
1 cup all-purpose flour	raisin liquid plus water
¾ cup sugar	to make ½ cup
1½ tsp. baking powder	1 egg
½ tsp. salt	2 tbsp. flour
1 tsp. cinnamon	½ cup chopped nuts
½ tsp. cloves	

Heat oven to 375° (quick mod.). Line 12 medium muffin cups with paper baking cups. Mix raisins and water in saucepan. Cover and simmer 15 min. Drain and save liquid. Measure flour by dipping method (p. 123) or by sifting. Stir flour, sugar, baking powder, salt, and spices in bowl. Add shortening and liquid. Beat 2 min. medium speed on mixer or 300 vigorous strokes by hand. Scrape sides and bottom of bowl constantly. Add egg. Beat 2 more min., scraping bowl frequently. Mix drained and cooled raisins with 2 additional tbsp. flour and nuts. Fold carefully into batter. Pour into baking cups, filling each about ½ full. Bake 15 to 20 min., or until toothpick inserted in center of cupcake comes out clean. Cupcakes may be served plain or iced with Browned Butter Icing (p. 35). *Makes 12 cupcakes.*

Note: Freeze extra cupcakes for serving at future meals or for lunch boxes.

Peach Short Pie Cobbler

⅓ to ½ cup sugar
1½ tsp. cornstarch
½ cup water

1½ cups sliced fresh
  peaches
Short Pie Rounds
  (below)

Mix sugar and cornstarch in saucepan. Gradually stir in water. Bring to boil; boil 1 min., stirring constantly. Add peaches. Pour into 2 individual serving dishes. Top with Short Pie Rounds. Serve warm. *2 servings.*

Note: Instead of fresh peaches, you may use 1 can (8 oz.) sliced peaches and ¼ cup sugar.

Full O' Boloney

1½ cups cubed raw
  potatoes (about
  1½ potatoes)
1½ cups cubed bologna
  (½ lb.)
2 tbsp. minced green
  pepper

1 can (10½ oz.) cream
  of celery soup,
  undiluted
2 large slices of
  cheese, quartered

Heat oven to 350° (mod.). Mix all ingredients except cheese in 1½-qt. baking dish. Bake covered 1 hr. 15 min. Remove cover; top with cheese. Broil until bubbly and browned. *4 servings.*

Leftovers? Cover and reheat in 350° (mod.) oven for another meal. Add 1 or 2 tbsp. milk, if needed.

Short Pie Rounds

Make these ahead of time.

Heat oven to 450° (hot). Add 1½ tbsp. boiling water to ½ cup buttermilk baking mix and 2 tbsp. butter in small bowl. Stir vigorously with fork until dough forms a ball and cleans the bowl. Dough will be puffy and soft. Divide into 4 parts. With palm of hand, flatten each part into a 3″ round on ungreased baking sheet. Prick with fork. Pinch edges to make more attractive. Bake about 8 min. *Makes 4 rounds.*

Leftover Short Pie Rounds? Wrap in waxed paper and refrigerate. Use the next day for another cobbler or as a topping for little meat pies.

Corned Beef Hash Supreme
Pineapple-Endive Salad
Ripe Olives   Celery Sticks
Pumpernickel Bread
Ice Cream with
Raspberry-Currant Sauce (p. 20)

Barleyburger Stew
Hot French Bread or Crackers
Lettuce Slices with Poppy Seed Dressing
Pineapple Upside-down Cake

Corned Beef Hash Supreme

1 clove garlic, minced	2 to 3 tbsp. water
¼ cup chopped onion	2 tbsp. minced
1 can (3 oz.) sliced	fresh parsley
mushrooms, drained	2 medium tomatoes,
1½ to 2 tbsp. butter	sliced ¼" thick
1 can (1 lb.) corned	grated Parmesan
beef hash, crumbled	cheese
⅓ cup commercial	
sour cream	

In small skillet, sauté garlic, onion, and mushrooms in butter until tender but not brown. Add hash; brown well, scraping bottom of pan frequently. Combine sour cream, water, and parsley; stir into hash mixture. Top with tomato slices. Cook, covered, over medium heat about 5 min., or until tomatoes are tender. Sprinkle with cheese; serve immediately, from skillet, if desired. *2 servings.*

Pineapple-Endive Salad

Insert a few small leaves of curly endive through the hole of each pineapple slice. (Allow 1 slice to a person.) Serve on large endive leaf with Oil-and-Vinegar Dressing (p. 59).

BE PENNYWISE

Look for a bottle of olive pieces when shopping. Use them in tossed salads, gelatin salads, and special casseroles, whenever you would be using cut-up slices.

Barleyburger Stew

¾ lb. ground beef	½ cup hot water
1 medium or 2 small	1½ tsp. chili powder
onions, chopped	1½ tsp. salt
2 tbsp. fat	¼ tsp. pepper
¼ cup chopped celery	¼ cup barley
2 cups tomato juice	

In large kettle brown beef and onions in hot fat, stirring frequently. Add remaining ingredients; cook slowly for 1 hr. *2 servings.*

Poppy Seed Dressing

2 tbsp. salad oil	dash of flavor enhancer
1 tbsp. vinegar	(monosodium
¾ tsp. salt	glutamate)
½ clove garlic, minced	¼ tsp. poppy seeds
ground fresh pepper	

Shake ingredients together in bottle. *Makes ¼ cup.*

Pineapple Upside-down Cake

3 tbsp. butter	pecan halves and
¼ cup brown sugar	maraschino cherries,
(packed)	if desired
3 drained pineapple	½ the batter for
slices	Dinette Cake (p. 62)

Grease sides of a loaf pan, 9x5x3". Melt butter in bottom of loaf pan. Sprinkle sugar evenly over butter. Arrange pineapple in attractive pattern on butter-sugar coating. Decorate with pecan halves and cherries if you wish. Pour the half batter over fruit (use the other half for Cupcakes, below).

Refrigerate unbaked Upside-down Cake while baking Cupcakes. Then lower oven temperature to 350° (mod.). Bake Upside-down Cake about 40 min., until toothpick stuck into center comes out clean. Immediately turn upside-down on serving plate. Leave pan on a few min. Serve warm with whipped cream.

Cupcakes

Use half of Dinette Cake batter (p. 62). Heat oven to 400° (mod. hot). Place paper cups or liners in 6 to 8 muffin cups. Fill cups ½ full of batter. Bake 18 to 20 min., or until done.

Hot Consommé
with Toasted Crackers
Hamburger Pie
Lettuce with Bohemian Club Dressing
Poppy Seed Rolls
Southern Ambrosia (p. 26)

Hot Consommé

Heat 1 can undiluted beef consommé or bouillon just to the boiling point. Serve hot. *2 servings.*

Toasted Crackers

Brush saltine crackers with salad oil or melted butter. Heat in 350° (mod.) oven until lightly browned. If desired, sprinkle buttered crackers with celery seeds, poppy seeds, or grated Parmesan cheese.

Hamburger Pie

2 tbsp. chopped onion	1 can (8 oz.) cut green beans, drained (1 cup)
1 tbsp. shortening	
½ lb. ground beef	
¼ tsp. salt	½ can tomato soup (10½-oz. can)
⅛ tsp. pepper	
¼ tsp. flavor enhancer (monosodium glutamate)	1 cup mashed potatoes (fresh, leftover, or instant) paprika

Heat oven to 350° (mod.). Cook onion in hot fat until yellow; add meat and cook until brown. Add seasonings, beans, and soup. Pour into 1-qt. baking dish. Spoon mashed potatoes over mixture. Sprinkle with paprika. Bake 30 min. *2 generous servings.*

Note: Dilute and heat remaining half-can of soup for lunch the next day.

Bohemian Club Dressing

Highly seasoned . . . a favorite with men. Has the consistency and appearance of Thousand Island Dressing.

cut clove of garlic	1 hard-cooked egg
¾ tsp. salt	2½ tbsp. vinegar
½ tsp. paprika	¼ cup plus 2 tbsp. vegetable oil
½ tsp. Worcestershire sauce	2 tbsp. chopped parsley
¼ tsp. dry mustard	¼ cup finely chopped green onion
¼ tsp. coarsely ground black pepper	

Rub a small bowl with garlic. Mix salt, paprika, Worcestershire sauce, mustard, and pepper in bowl. Mash hard-cooked egg yolk into seasonings. Stir in vinegar, oil, chopped egg white, parsley, and onion. Serve over lettuce. Refrigerate remaining dressing. *Makes ¾ cup.*

Note: To save time and work, use bottled Thousand Island Dressing.

BE PENNYWISE

Compare prices when shopping. Remember which stores have special values on certain items.

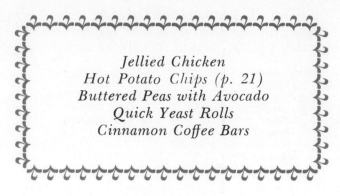

Jellied Chicken
Hot Potato Chips (p. 21)
Buttered Peas with Avocado
Quick Yeast Rolls
Cinnamon Coffee Bars

Jellied Chicken

Cooked veal, beef, or lamb may be used in place of chicken . . . hot meat stock or bouillon in place of chicken broth.

1 envelope unflavored gelatin (1 tbsp.)	2 tbsp. sliced pimiento-stuffed green olives
1¾ cups chicken broth	1 tbsp. minced onion
2 cups cut-up cooked chicken	½ tsp. salt
2 tbsp. lemon juice	pimiento
¼ cup chopped celery	tomato wedges

Soften gelatin in ½ cup cold broth. Heat and stir over low heat until gelatin dissolves. Stir in remaining broth. Chill until partially set. Mix remaining ingredients except pimiento and tomato wedges; fold into gelatin. Pour into 9x5x3″ loaf pan or 1-qt. refrigerator tray. Chill until set. Unmold on chilled platter. Serve cold garnished with pimiento and tomato wedges. *4 servings.*

Buttered Peas with Avocado

Prepare Buttered Peas using 1 pkg. frozen peas. Just before serving, toss with strips or cubes of peeled avocado. (A whole avocado should be just right.)

Quick Yeast Rolls

1 pkg. active dry yeast	2 tbsp. shortening
⅔ cup warm water (not hot—110 to 115°)	2½ cups buttermilk baking mix
2 tbsp. sugar	melted butter

Dissolve yeast in water. Stir in sugar, shortening, and baking mix; beat vigorously. Turn dough onto surface well dusted with baking mix. Knead until smooth, about 20 times. Shape as desired, into crescents, rolls, etc. Place on lightly greased baking sheet. Cover with damp cloth. Let rise in warm place (85°) until double, about 30 min. Heat oven to 400° (mod. hot). Bake 10 to 15 min., depending on size. Brush with melted butter after baking. *Makes 16 rolls.*

Cinnamon Coffee Bars

¼ cup soft shortening	¼ tsp. soda
1 cup brown sugar (packed)	¼ tsp. salt
1 egg	½ tsp. cinnamon
½ cup hot coffee	½ cup seedless raisins
1½ cups all-purpose flour	¼ cup chopped nuts
1 tsp. baking powder	Quick Cream Icing (below)

Heat oven to 350° (mod.). Cream shortening, sugar, and egg; stir in coffee. Mix dry ingredients and stir in. Blend in raisins and nuts. Spread in greased and floured oblong pan, 13x9½x2″. Bake 18 to 20 min. Cut into 3x1½″ bars. Frost while warm with thin coating of Quick Cream Icing. *Makes 2 doz. bars.*

Quick Cream Icing: Mix ¾ cup sifted confectioners' sugar, ¼ tsp. vanilla, and about 1 tbsp. cream.

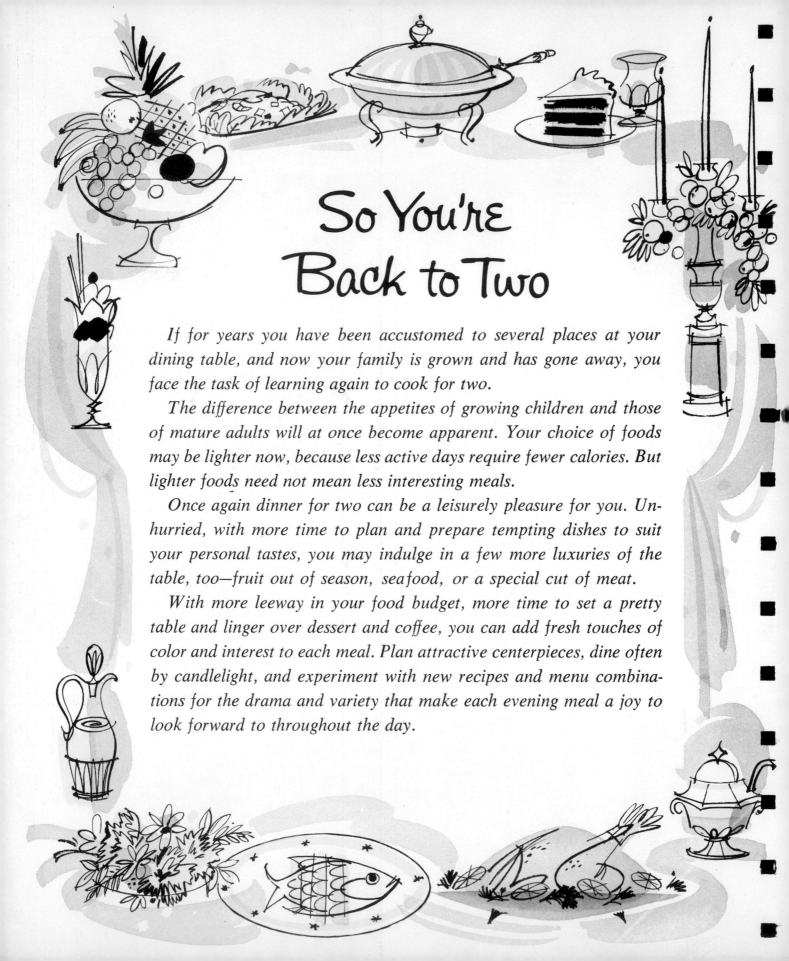

So You're Back to Two

If for years you have been accustomed to several places at your dining table, and now your family is grown and has gone away, you face the task of learning again to cook for two.

The difference between the appetites of growing children and those of mature adults will at once become apparent. Your choice of foods may be lighter now, because less active days require fewer calories. But lighter foods need not mean less interesting meals.

Once again dinner for two can be a leisurely pleasure for you. Unhurried, with more time to plan and prepare tempting dishes to suit your personal tastes, you may indulge in a few more luxuries of the table, too—fruit out of season, seafood, or a special cut of meat.

With more leeway in your food budget, more time to set a pretty table and linger over dessert and coffee, you can add fresh touches of color and interest to each meal. Plan attractive centerpieces, dine often by candlelight, and experiment with new recipes and menu combinations for the drama and variety that make each evening meal a joy to look forward to throughout the day.

Hot Consommé
Salisbury Steak with Mushroom Gravy
Parsleyed Rice
Green Peas with Tiny Pearl Onions
Mandarin Orange Gelatin Rings
Floating Island

Salisbury Steak with Mushroom Gravy

1 lb. ground round steak or ground beef	2 tbsp. fat or vegetable oil
¼ tsp. pepper	Mushroom Gravy
1 tsp. salt	(below)

Combine meat, pepper, and salt. Shape into 3 or 4 plump oval patties. Pan-fry in hot fat in a skillet or broil 4 to 6 min. each side. Serve with Mushroom Gravy. *2 generous servings.*

Mushroom Gravy

¼ cup sliced mushrooms or 1 can (2 oz.) mushrooms	2 tbsp. flour
	1 cup water
	1 beef bouillon cube

Remove meat patties to a warm plate. Pan-fry mushrooms in the drippings. Add flour to drippings in pan; stir. Add water and bouillon cube. Cook until mixture boils, cube is dissolved, and sauce is thickened. Pour over patties.

Parsleyed Rice

Toss Fluffy White Rice (p. 26) with minced parsley.

Mandarin Orange Gelatin Rings

1 pkg. (3 oz.) orange-flavored gelatin	½ pt. orange sherbet
	1 can (11 oz.) mandarin oranges, drained
1 cup boiling liquid (water or fruit juice)	

Dissolve gelatin in boiling liquid. Immediately add orange sherbet and stir until melted. Pour into individual ring molds and chill until firm. Unmold on lettuce leaf and fill center with chilled orange slices. Top with maraschino cherry. *5 to 6 servings.*

Note: This keeps beautifully for another meal.

Floating Island

Make Soft Custard (below). Make a meringue of 1 egg white and 2 tbsp. sugar. Drop meringue as "islands" on custard in serving dish. Chill before serving.

Soft Custard

¾ cup milk	2 tbsp. sugar
2 egg yolks (or 1 whole egg)	pinch of salt
	½ tsp. vanilla

Scald milk in top of double boiler over direct heat. Beat egg yolks in small bowl. Blend in sugar and salt. Gradually stir in scalded milk. Return to double boiler. Cook over simmering (not boiling) water, stirring constantly. When custard coats silver spoon (thin coating), remove from heat. Cool quickly. If custard should start to curdle, beat vigorously at once with rotary beater until smooth. Blend in vanilla. Pour into serving dish. *2 generous servings.*

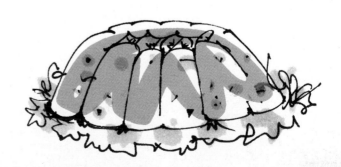

Tomato Bouillon
Baked Meat Balls
Scalloped Potatoes (p. 18)
Beets in Orange Sauce
Green Pea and Cheese Salad
Pineapple Marshmallow Cream

Tomato Bouillon

Heat together equal amounts of chicken bouillon (canned or cubes) and tomato juice with 3 or 4 whole cloves. Garnish with thin lemon slices. (If using bouillon cubes, use 1 cube to ½ cup water and 1 cup tomato juice.)

Baked Meat Balls

1 egg	1½ slices bread, cubed
¼ cup milk	1 tsp. salt
1½ tsp. instant minced onion	⅛ tsp. pepper
	1 lb. ground beef

Heat oven to 350° (mod.). Beat egg and milk. Stir in onion, bread, and seasonings. Add beef and mix well. Shape into balls, using ⅓ cup mixture for each ball. Place in shallow pan. Bake 30 to 40 min. *Makes about 7 meat balls.*

Beets in Orange Sauce

1½ tsp. butter	dash of salt and pepper
2 tbsp. brown sugar or granulated sugar	1 can (8 oz.) diced beets, drained (1 cup)
½ tsp. cornstarch	
⅓ cup orange juice	

Melt butter. Mix sugar and cornstarch; blend into butter. Stir in orange juice and cook until thickened, stirring constantly. Add salt, pepper, and beets. Cook until beets are heated through. Sprinkle with grated orange rind, if desired. *2 servings.*

Green Pea and Cheese Salad

¾ cup cooked peas	2 tbsp. mayonnaise
¼ cup diced Cheddar cheese	¾ tsp. prepared mustard
1 tbsp. finely chopped onion	

Combine peas, cheese, and onion. Toss with mayonnaise and mustard. Chill. Serve on greens. *2 servings.*

Pineapple Marshmallow Cream

1 can (8¾ oz.) crushed pineapple (about 1 cup)	2 cups miniature marshmallows
1 tbsp. lemon juice	½ cup whipping cream, whipped

Combine crushed pineapple, lemon juice, and marshmallows in saucepan. Place over low heat; stir until marshmallows are dissolved. Remove from heat; cool. When partially set, fold in whipped cream. Spoon into sherbet dishes and chill 2 hr. or overnight. *4 servings.*

Leftover Pineapple Cream? Refrigerate and serve another day—just as delicious.

Saucy Pork 'N Noodle Bake
Stewed Tomatoes   Hard Rolls
Blueberry Sundae Shortcake

Saucy Pork 'N Noodle Bake

1 cup cubed cooked pork	1 can (8 oz.) whole-kernel corn, undrained
1 tbsp. shortening	1 tbsp. sliced pimiento
½ cup narrow noodles, uncooked	½ cup shredded sharp Cheddar cheese
1 can (10½ oz.) cream of chicken soup	¼ cup finely diced green pepper

Heat oven to 375° (quick mod.). Brown meat in melted shortening in skillet. When meat is well browned, drain excess fat from skillet; add remaining ingredients and mix. Pour into 1-qt. casserole; bake 45 min., stirring occasionally. *2 generous servings.*

Stewed Tomatoes

Simmer together 10 min.: 1¾ cups cooked tomatoes, ½ tsp. minced onion, ¾ tsp. sugar, 1 tbsp. butter, ¼ cup soft bread cubes, and dash of pepper. *2 servings.*

Blueberry Sundae Shortcake

Place scoop of ice cream (vanilla, peach, or blueberry ripple) on slice of unfrosted white, yellow, pound, or sponge cake or on split-open cupcake. Top with Blueberry Sauce (below).

Blueberry Sauce

1 cup blueberries	¼ cup sugar
2 tbsp. water	¼ tsp. cinnamon

Combine ingredients in saucepan. Bring to a boil and cook 5 min., stirring occasionally. Serve warm over ice cream and cake. *Makes about ⅔ cup.*

Eggs Delmonico
Lemon-buttered Carrots
Sliced Orange-Endive Salad
Peach Melba

Eggs Delmonico

1 can (10½ oz.) cream of mushroom soup	4 hard-cooked eggs, cut in quarters
½ tbsp. minced pimiento	2 slices toast paprika
¼ cup grated cheese	parsley

Heat soup over low heat. Stir in pimiento and cheese. Carefully fold in eggs. Continue cooking over low heat until cheese is melted. Serve immediately on hot buttered toast; sprinkle with paprika and garnish with parsley. *2 generous servings.*

Whole Carrots

Wash and scrape 4 or 5 young carrots. Cook, covered, in 1″ boiling salted water 15 to 20 min., until tender. Drain; serve with butter, salt, and pepper or brush with Lemon Butter (below). *2 servings.*

Lemon Butter

Melt 2 tbsp. butter. Blend in 1 tbsp. lemon juice and ½ tsp. grated lemon rind.

Sliced Orange-Endive Salad

Peel and slice 1 orange. Arrange slices on endive or other greens. If you wish, serve with a fruit dressing such as 1-2-3 Fruit Dressing (p. 89) or Sweet French Dressing (p. 29).

Peach Melba

Place a peach half on a mound of vanilla ice cream. Top with Raspberry-Currant Sauce (p. 20).

...and more egg dishes

Baked Eggs on Corned Beef Hash

Use canned hash or homemade (p. 104) for this quick supper dish.

Spread 2 cups warmed moist corned beef hash in well-greased shallow baking dish. Make deep hollows in hash. Dot each with butter and break an egg into it. Season with salt and pepper; cover with 1 tbsp. cream. Bake in 400° (mod. hot) oven 15 to 20 min., until eggs are set. Serve at once. *2 servings.*

Eggs Benedict

Try this New Orleans specialty for a delightful brunch, luncheon, or supper.

For each serving, butter a round of split and toasted English Muffin (or toast), then cover with a thin slice of fried ham (same size) or spread with deviled ham. Top each with a poached egg and cover with Hollandaise Sauce (below). Serve at once.

Hollandaise Sauce

Remember to keep heat low and stir sauce briskly all the time.

2 egg yolks	½ cup very cold butter
3 tbsp. lemon juice	(1 stick or ¼ lb.)

In small saucepan, stir together egg yolks and lemon juice with wooden spoon. Add half of butter (½ stick). Stir over very low heat until butter is melted. Add rest of butter. Continue stirring until butter is melted and sauce thickened. (Be sure butter melts slowly as this gives eggs time to cook and thicken the sauce without curdling.) Serve hot or at room temperature. If sauce separates, heat while slowly stirring in 1 tsp. water. *Makes 1 cup.*

Leftover Sauce? Keep in the refrigerator. To serve, stir in a little hot water.

Creamed Eggs

Another quickly made main dish with hard-cooked eggs. Delicious when served with Canadian bacon.

3 hard-cooked eggs	1 cup well-seasoned Medium White Sauce (p. 122)

Cut eggs in quarters; add to White Sauce. Serve hot over hot buttered toast strips, crisp chow mein noodles, or fluffy boiled rice. Sprinkle with paprika. Garnish with parsley sprigs. *2 servings.*

Lamb Shish-Kabobs
Green Rice
Bean Salad
Applemint Ripple Ice Cream

Lamb Shish-Kabobs

¾ lb. lamb shoulder or shank, cut into 1″ cubes	¼ to ½ tsp. oregano
	½ cup pineapple chunks
½ small onion, thinly sliced	½ large onion, cut in 1″ pieces
¾ tsp. salt	1 firm tomato, cut in 1″ wedges
⅛ tsp. coarsely ground pepper	1 tbsp. vegetable oil

Place lamb cubes in a bowl. Tuck in onion slices. Add seasonings. Refrigerate 1 to 2 hr. Alternate meat cubes, chunks of pineapple, onion, and tomato on metal skewers. Roll in vegetable oil. Broil 3″ from heat, about 15 to 20 min. Turn as meats and vegetables brown. *2 servings.*

Green Rice

½ cup plus 1 tbsp. instant rice	¼ cup finely chopped parsley
¼ cup commercial sour cream	1½ tsp. grated onion

Cook rice as directed on pkg. Mix all ingredients. Season to taste. Heat. *2 servings.*

Bean Salad

1 cup drained cooked kidney beans	¼ tsp. salt
	pinch of pepper
2 tbsp. diced celery	about 2 tbsp.
2 pickles (dill or sweet), chopped	mayonnaise or commercial sour cream
1 tbsp. minced onion	grated cheese
1 hard-cooked egg, sliced	

Mix all ingredients except mayonnaise. Then mix lightly with mayonnaise. Chill thoroughly. Serve on salad greens. Garnish with grated cheese. *2 servings.*

Applemint Ripple Ice Cream

½ cup applesauce red or green food coloring	¼ tsp. peppermint extract
	1 pt. vanilla ice cream, softened

Tint applesauce deep pink or mint green. Mix in peppermint extract. Spread half the ice cream in refrigerator tray. Swirl half the applesauce into ice cream. Spread remaining ice cream on top; swirl in remaining applesauce. Freeze just until firm. Serve in dessert dishes; garnish with mint leaf or maraschino cherry. *2 servings.*

TO USE PARFAIT GLASSES
Layer applesauce with ice cream in parfait glasses, beginning with ice cream and finishing with applesauce. Freeze just until firm. Garnish with mint leaf or maraschino cherry.

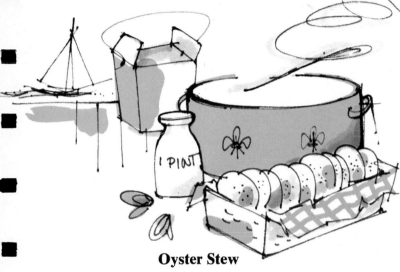

Oyster Stew

2 cups milk
½ cup cream
¼ cup butter
1 pint oysters, with the liquor
1 tsp. salt
dash of pepper

Heat milk and cream to scalding. Just before serving, melt butter in saucepan. Add oysters with liquor; cook gently, just until oyster edges curl. Add to scalded milk and cream. Season with salt and pepper. Serve immediately. Offer oyster or other crackers. *2 servings*.

HOW TO GRILL SANDWICHES
Make sandwiches. Brush lightly with melted butter or spread with soft butter on both sides; heat until golden brown in heavy skillet or electric grill.

Mince Pie

Prepare Tender-flaky Pastry for 8″ Two-crust Pie (p. 126). Line pie pan. Mix 2 cups mincemeat (19-oz. jar or 9-oz. pkg.) with 1 cup chopped apple. Heat oven to 425° (hot). Pour filling into pastry-lined pie pan. Cover with top crust which has slits in it. Bake 40 to 45 min., until crust is nicely browned. Serve while warm.

Hot Beef Sandwiches

Heat oven to 400° (mod. hot). Place slices of leftover roast beef in buttered bun or between slices of buttered bread. Wrap tightly in aluminum foil; bake 15 min., or until heated through. Serve plain, or with catsup, hot mustard, or leftover gravy.

Garden Dew Dressing

¼ cup vegetable oil
2 tbsp. vinegar
1½ tsp. finely chopped chives or 1 tbsp. finely chopped onion
2 tbsp. fresh minced parsley
1½ tsp. finely chopped green pepper
½ tsp. sugar
¼ tsp. salt
½ tsp. dry mustard
dash of red pepper

Shake all ingredients well in a tightly covered jar. Keep in covered jar in refrigerator. Just before serving, shake again to blend. *Makes about ½ cup.*

Cinnamon-Blueberry Sauce

1 cup fresh or frozen blueberries
2 tbsp. water
2 tbsp. sugar
1 tbsp. lemon juice
1 tsp. cornstarch
¼ tsp. cinnamon

Blend ingredients in saucepan. Bring to a boil; simmer 5 min., stirring occasionally. Serve warm over ice cream. *Makes about ⅔ cup.*

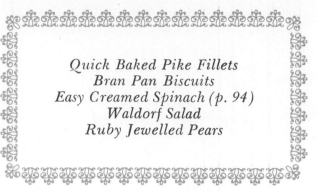

Quick Baked Pike Fillets
Bran Pan Biscuits
Easy Creamed Spinach (p. 94)
Waldorf Salad
Ruby Jewelled Pears

Quick Baked Pike Fillets

3/4 to 1 lb. dressed pike fillets	flour or buttermilk baking mix
salt and pepper	1 tbsp. butter, melted

Heat oven to 500° (very hot). Season fish with salt and pepper. Dip in flour or baking mix. Place fish in lightly greased baking pan. Drizzle with butter. Sprinkle with paprika, if desired. Bake 10 to 15 min., or until done. Serve immediately, garnished with tomato and lemon wedges. *2 servings.*

Bran Pan Biscuits

1 pkg. active dry yeast	1½ tsp. salt
1 cup warm water (not hot—110 to 115°)	½ cup whole bran or rolled oats
3½ to 3¾ cups all-purpose flour	1 egg
¼ cup brown sugar (packed)	3 tbsp. soft shortening

In mixing bowl, dissolve yeast in water. Measure flour by dipping method (p. 123) or by sifting. Stir half of flour and remaining ingredients into yeast. Stir with spoon until smooth. Add just enough flour until easy to handle. Mix with hand. Place dough in greased bowl, turning once to bring greased side up. Cover with cloth; let rise in warm place (85°) until double, about 1½ hr. Shape dough into balls ⅓ of size desired. Place close together in a greased round pan. Flour or grease fingers while shaping as dough is sticky. Cover and let rise until double, about 45 min. Heat oven to 375° (quick mod.). Bake 20 to 25 min. *Makes about 2 doz. biscuits.*

Leftover Biscuits? Wrap in foil; reheat and serve for brunch the following day.

Waldorf Salad

1 cup diced apple (red skin on)	¼ cup mayonnaise or 2 or 3 tbsp. mayonnaise thinned with cream
½ cup diced celery a few broken nuts	

Lightly mix apple, celery, and nuts. Toss with mayonnaise. Serve in lettuce cups. For a perky finish, top each serving with a maraschino cherry. *2 servings.*

Ruby Jewelled Pears

1 can (1 lb.) whole cranberry sauce	¼ cup sugar
¼ tsp. cinnamon	4 fresh pears, peeled and cored from blossom end
2 tbsp. lemon juice	

Heat oven to 350° (mod.). Stir cranberry sauce, cinnamon, lemon juice, and sugar over low heat until well blended and sugar is melted. Stand pears in baking dish; pour the prepared cranberry sauce over them. Bake 30 min., or until tender, basting occasionally. Serve warm or chilled with whipped cream. *4 servings.*

Leftover Jewelled Pears? These can be served the next day as a meat accompaniment.

Baby Beef Liver and Onions
Mashed Potato Cakes
Tomato-Vegetable Aspic
Extra-quick Butter Sticks
Your Favorite Sherbet

Baby Beef Liver and Onions

Peel and slice 2 medium sweet onions. Cook in hot bacon fat until golden. Cover and cook slowly until tender. Season with salt and pepper. Remove to warm plate and keep warm.

Dip ½″-thick slices of liver (¼ lb. each) in flour. Brown in hot fat; season. Cook over low heat 10 to 15 min., turning once. Serve hot topped with onions. *2 servings.*

Mashed Potato Cakes

Shape fluffy Mashed Potatoes (p. 36) into cakes or form into a roll; wrap in waxed paper; chill; slice. Dip into flour. Fry slowly in hot fat until brown.

Extra-Quick Butter Sticks

Heat oven to 450° (hot). Melt ¼ cup butter. Pour half into a square pan, 8x8x2″. Roll unbaked biscuits from 1 can refrigerated biscuits, twisting to about 8″ lengths. Place in pan. Pour rest of butter over tops. Sprinkle with caraway, poppy, celery, or sesame seeds. Bake 8 to 10 min., until golden brown. Let stand in pan about 2 min. to absorb butter. *Makes 10 sticks.*

Leftover Butter Sticks? Wrap in foil; reheat in 375° oven for 20 min.

Tomato-Vegetable Aspic

1 envelope unflavored gelatin (1 tbsp.)	½ bay leaf, crumbled
¼ cup cold water	1 small onion, cut up
1 cup tomato juice	a few celery leaves
½ tsp. salt	1½ tsp. lemon juice
½ tsp. confectioners' sugar	½ cup diced celery
dash each of cayenne pepper and celery salt	¼ cup chopped bread-and-butter pickles

Soften gelatin in water. Simmer tomato juice, seasonings, onion, and celery leaves together for 15 min. Strain and add softened gelatin and lemon juice, stirring until dissolved. Cool. Add diced celery and pickles. Pour into 2 individual molds. Chill until firm. Unmold on salad greens and serve with mayonnaise. *2 servings.*

BE PENNYWISE

Take a tip from the gourmets. Herbs and spices can do wonders with economy meat cuts. A gay garnish adds eye appeal. Try a pickled beet or crabapple, slices of orange, or little bunches of grapes.

Good Foods for Less Active Two-somes

Meats, Poultry, and Fish
Breaded Veal Chops, p. 9
Roast Beef, p. 20
Roast Leg of Lamb, p. 30
Roast Chicken or Turkey, p. 51
Minute Steaks, p. 69
Salmon Loaf, p. 69
Broiled Lamb Chops, p. 71
Meat Loaf, p. 94

Main Dishes
Dried Beef Rarebit, p. 54
Cheese Soufflé, p. 62
Chicken Caruso, p. 68
Chicken à la King, p. 72
Quick Trick Chicken and Rice, p. 73
Shepherd's Pie, p. 74
Puffy Omelet, p. 76
Glorified Egg Shortcake, p. 92
Old-fashioned Vegetable Soup, p. 97
Macaroni and Cheese, p. 99

Breads
Dark Date Nut Bread, p. 11
Anadama Bread, p. 24
Poppy Seed Sticks, p. 54
Popovers, p. 85
Herb Bread, p. 124

Salads
Molded Lime-Pineapple Salad, p. 18
Blushing Pear Salad, p. 42
Festival Peach Salad, p. 96
Mexican Green Bean Salad, p. 99

Vegetables
Double-deck Potatoes and Carrots, p. 9
Baked Squash, p. 22
Creamed Asparagus, p. 25
Green Beans and Corn, p. 32
Creamed Onions, p. 51
Minted Peas, p. 71
Broiled Zucchini, p. 73
Easy Creamed Spinach, p. 94
Lemon-buttered Carrots, p. 113

Desserts
Portia's Pears, p. 14
Fruited Gelatin, p. 25
Southern Ambrosia, p. 26
Rhubarb Sauce, p. 30
Baked Bananas, p. 50
Fruit with Whipped Topping, p. 69
Plum Cobbler, p. 78
Prune or Apricot Whip, p. 79
Tapioca Cream, p. 82
Baked Peach Halves, p. 96

Sunset Years Guide

• Serve some protein, whether as cereals, lean meats, dried peas or beans, at all three meals daily.
• Stress liquids: cups of bouillon or consommé, fruit and vegetable juices as snacks, milk shakes, milk punches, and frosty fruit-ades.
• Step up vitamins and minerals with liver, egg yolks, yellow and green leafy vegetables, citrus fruit or dried fruits in each day's meals.
• Keep calcium supply high with creamed foods, custards, cheeses, and ice cream.
• Limit the use of salt; instead try herbs or spices.
• Include easy-to-eat foods like gelatin salads, soufflés, and mashed potatoes.

• Avoid foods containing much roughage, such as cabbage, celery, and whole kernel corn.
• Contrast crisp-textured foods like toast points, crackers, and chow mein noodles with softer foods in a menu.
• Substitute foods that are filling but low in calories for those high in fats and carbohydrates: a hearty vegetable like acorn squash for potatoes, a light chiffon pie in place of cream pie or cake.
• Remember that variety is the spice of interesting meals. Include new foods or new versions of well-liked foods along with those which have been favorites since childhood.

Cook's Primer

Roasting a fine cut of beef to perfection or creating a salad that tastes every bit as good as it looks is an art. And the creative cook, like any artist or craftsman, can be no better than the basic techniques she has mastered.

The abc's of cooking and marketing that follow on these pages were written especially for you—the new bride, the career girl enjoying her first apartment, or the experienced homemaker welcoming a little refresher course. Included are methods and guides which will help you plan your menus, glamorize your favorite dishes, and work wonders with the "foundation foods" of good day-to-day meals.

Here, too, you will find marketing help on food buying for two and stocking the emergency shelf, as well as a handy checklist of essential kitchen equipment to help you be prepared for all kinds of cooking occasions.

This, then, is your brief guide to managing a convenient, happy kitchen and, we hope, to good cooking always.

Helpful Hints for Gravy

For Smooth, Lump-free Gravy

Measure fat and flour accurately. Too much flour makes gravy lumpy and too thick; too much fat makes gravy greasy and separated.

Combine flour with other ingredients properly to separate the flour granules and keep them from lumping. In Pan Gravy, blend the fat and flour into a smooth paste; cook until it bubbles; stir in liquid gradually. In Kettle Gravy, shake or stir flour with cold water until *all* lumps are gone before adding it to hot liquid gradually.

For Well-flavored Gravy

Pan Gravy: Let the amount of brown drippings—not fat—determine the amount of gravy you make. Drippings are juices and small pieces of meat that brown and cook onto the pan during roasting. If short of brown drippings, add butter to drippings in roasting pan; brown. The more gravy you make from the same amount of drippings, the less flavor it will have. One cup of gravy is a good amount for a 3-lb. roast; ½ cup for steaks, chops, or fried chicken.

Kettle Gravy: Keep the amount of cooking liquid small—the less liquid in which you cook the meat, the better the gravy will taste. One-half cup of liquid is just right for a 2-lb. pot roast. (This won't cook dry in a heavy, tightly covered pan in the oven or over low top-of-the-range heat. If more water is needed, keep amount to less than ½ cup.) For stew, use 2 cups for 1 lb. meat. This larger amount is needed to cover the meat, but the vegetables and seasonings add to the flavor of the gravy.

Add Flavor Boosters: Cook meat with seasonings such as bay leaf, peppercorns, onion, garlic, celery salt, or other favorites. Add a bouillon cube of either chicken or beef. Try a variety of liquids, such as potato water, water from cooked mild vegetables, consommé, cream, sour cream, milk, tomato, or vegetable juice.

If Gravy Turns out Less than Perfect

If gravy has lumps:
   Pour through a strainer before serving.

If gravy is too greasy:
   Skim a paper towel across gravy or
   Skim gravy with a lettuce leaf or
   Wrap ice cube in cheesecloth; skim gravy.

If gravy lacks color:
   Add a dash of bottled gravy coloring.

Pan Gravy

Rich in the natural meat drippings left in the pan after cooking roasts, steaks, chops, and fried chicken.

For each cup of Medium Gravy use:

2 tbsp. fat	1 cup liquid (water,
2 tbsp. flour	meat stock, or
	bouillon cube broth)

For each cup of Thin Gravy use:

1 tbsp. fat	1 cup liquid (water,
1 tbsp. flour	meat stock, or
	bouillon cube broth)

Remove meat to warm place. Pour off clear fat (not drippings); measure amount needed into small saucepan. Measure liquid into roasting pan; stir and scrape all of brown drippings loose from pan—heat mixture if necessary; set aside.

Add flour to fat in saucepan; stir together until smooth. Cook over low heat, stirring steadily until it is bubbling.

Take pan off heat. Gradually stir in liquid and drippings from roasting pan. Return pan to heat; bring to boil, stirring constantly. Boil 1 min. Season and serve.

Kettle Gravy

Made from the liquid in which pot roasts and stews have been simmered.

For each cup of Medium Gravy use:

1 cup meat broth	2 tbsp. flour
¼ cup cold water	

For each cup of Thin Gravy use:

1 cup meat broth	1 tbsp. flour
¼ cup cold water	

Remove meat to platter; keep warm. Skim excess fat from meat broth. Pour off broth; measure amount needed; return to kettle.

Shake water and flour together in covered jar until all lumps are gone. For a smooth mixture, put water in first, flour on top.

Stir flour and water slowly into hot broth. Bring to boil, stirring constantly. Boil 1 min. Season and serve.

Creamy Gravy

Follow the directions for making Pan or Kettle Gravy —except use milk for part of liquid.

White Sauce

For Thin White Sauce (like coffee cream):
Used for creamed vegetables and soups.

1 tbsp. butter	⅛ tsp. pepper
½ to 1 tbsp. flour	1 cup milk
¼ tsp. salt	

For Medium White Sauce (like thick cream):
Used for creamed and scalloped dishes.

2 tbsp. butter	⅛ tsp. pepper
2 tbsp. flour	1 cup milk
¼ tsp. salt	

For Thick White Sauce (like batter):
Used for croquettes and soufflés.

¼ cup butter	⅛ tsp. pepper
¼ cup all-purpose flour	1 cup milk
¼ tsp. salt	

Melt butter over low heat in a heavy saucepan. (Wooden spoon for stirring is a help.)

Blend in flour and seasonings. Cook over low heat, stirring until mixture is smooth and bubbly.

Remove from heat. Stir in milk. Bring to boil, stirring constantly. Boil 1 min. *Makes 1 cup.*

Short Cut to White Sauce

Make a roux (butter paste) by blending to a smooth paste equal amounts of soft butter and flour; refrigerate in a covered jar. To get the consistency of sauce desired, blend the amount of roux indicated below into 1 cup of scalded milk or other liquid.

For thin sauce . . . 1½ tbsp. roux
For medium sauce . . . 3 tbsp. roux
For thick sauce . . . 4½ tbsp. roux

Add salt, pepper, and desired seasoning. Stir constantly until mixture boils. Boil 1 min. Remove from heat.

Cheese Sauce

For vegetable, rice, macaroni, and egg dishes.

Make 1 cup Medium White Sauce (above)—except add ¼ tsp. dry mustard with the seasonings. Blend in ½ cup nippy Cheddar cheese (cut up or grated). Stir until cheese is melted.

Mushroom Sauce

Make 1 cup Medium White Sauce (above)—except sauté 1 cup sliced mushrooms and 1 tsp. grated onion in the butter 5 min. before adding flour.

Rich Cheese Sauce

Make 1 cup Medium White Sauce (left)—except add 1 cup cut up or grated nippy Cheddar cheese, 1 tsp. dry mustard, ½ tsp. Worcestershire sauce. Stir until cheese is melted.

Cucumber Sauce

Refreshing with salmon and other fish.

Make 1 cup Medium White Sauce (left)—except add ½ cup cucumber, grated or thinly sliced, and a dash of cayenne pepper. Simmer 10 min.

Curry Sauce

Perfect with chicken, lamb, or shrimp and rice.

Make 1 cup Medium White Sauce (left)—except sauté ½ tsp. curry powder in the butter before adding flour and other seasoning.

Dill Sauce

An ideal mate for bland meat or fish.

Make 1 cup Medium White Sauce (left)—except with the seasonings, add 1 tsp. minced fresh dill or ½ tsp. dried dill and a dash of nutmeg. Simmer 2 or 3 min.

Egg Sauce

A pleasant addition to salmon and other fish.

Make 1 cup Medium White Sauce (left)—except carefully stir in 2 diced hard-cooked eggs. Season.

Mustard Sauce

Make 1 cup Medium White Sauce (left)—except add 1 tbsp. prepared mustard.

Horseradish Sauce

Make 1 cup Medium White Sauce (left)—except add ⅓ cup bottled horseradish, ¼ tsp. dry mustard, and a dash of paprika.

Velvet Sauce

Make 1 cup Medium White Sauce (left)—except use chicken, veal, or fish stock in place of milk. Add ⅛ tsp. nutmeg.

Helpful Hints for Biscuits

• Be sure the oven is hot (450°) throughout the baking period. A lower temperature will dry biscuits out before they are done.
• Avoid adding extra flour or buttermilk baking mix to the dough, by using a pastry set when kneading and rolling out biscuits. Or use a heavy canvas-like cloth over your board and a stockinet cover over your rolling pin. Flour or baking mix rubbed into the covers will keep the dough from sticking, yet it will not be absorbed by the dough to toughen it.
• A heavy or shiny baking sheet will help prevent over-browning biscuits on the bottom.
• Save time in cutting by patting out dough on baking sheet. Cut into squares with a sharp knife.
• If you want soft sides, place biscuits close together on baking sheet.
• If you want crusty sides, place biscuits on baking sheet with spaces between.
• Serve biscuits piping hot from the oven. Put them in a napkin in a serving dish to retain the heat. Replenish from the oven as you need more.

Rolled Biscuits

1 cup all-purpose flour	2 tbsp. shortening
1½ tsp. baking powder	¼ cup plus 2 tbsp. milk
½ tsp. salt	

Heat oven to 450° (hot). Measure flour by dipping method (right) or by sifting. Mix dry ingredients well in bowl. Cut in shortening with pastry blender until mixture looks like "meal." Stir in milk.

Round up on lightly floured cloth-covered board. Knead lightly 20 to 25 times.

Roll dough or pat out to about ½″ thickness. Cut close together with floured biscuit cutter. Place on ungreased baking sheet. Bake 10 to 12 min. *Makes ten 1¾″ biscuits.*

Note: For richer biscuits, increase shortening to 3 tbsp. and decrease milk to ⅓ cup.

Quick Biscuits

Heat oven to 450° (hot). Make Biscuit dough as directed on buttermilk baking mix pkg.—except use ½ the amounts of ingredients.

Roll dough around on cloth-covered board lightly dusted with flour to prevent sticking. Knead gently 8 to 10 times to smooth dough.

Roll out ½″ thick. (Biscuits double in thickness in baking.) Dip cutter in flour. Cut close together to save rerolling.

Place on ungreased shiny baking sheet. Bake 10 to 12 min., until golden brown. Serve immediately. *Makes six 2″ biscuits.*

Note: For richer biscuits, stir in with the liquid 2 tbsp. shortening.

Drop Biscuits

Heat oven to 450° (hot). Make dough for Rolled (left) or Quick (above) Biscuits—except instead of rounding up on cloth-covered board, drop with spoon onto greased baking sheet. Bake 10 to 15 min., until golden brown.

Measuring Flour by the Dipping Method

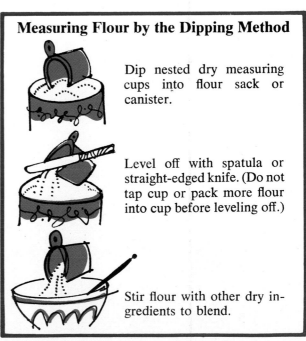

Dip nested dry measuring cups into flour sack or canister.

Level off with spatula or straight-edged knife. (Do not tap cup or pack more flour into cup before leveling off.)

Stir flour with other dry ingredients to blend.

Helpful Hints for Yeast Breads

• Dissolve yeast at the correct temperature: active dry yeast at 110 to 115° (very warm to the touch), compressed yeast at 80 to 85° (slightly cool). Hot temperatures kill yeast, cold temperatures slow its growth. The mixing bowl can be rinsed in hot water, and all other ingredients should be the proper temperature before being mixed with the yeast.

• Use the right amount of flour for the best texture. Add the second addition of flour just until the dough cleans the bowl. Then as you knead, sprinkle flour little by little into dough just until it no longer sticks to hands or board.

• Knead dough by folding it in half towards you, then pressing it down and pushing it away. Kneading gives dough the ability to stretch and expand as it rises.

• Keep rising dough away from drafts and at a temperature of 85°. If too warm, bread will be dark, coarse, and taste "yeasty." If too cool, bread will be heavy and solid. If kitchen is cool, place bowl of dough on rack over a bowl of hot water and cover completely with a towel.

• Dough has risen enough when it retains the impression after being lightly touched.

• Punching down the dough and letting it rise a second time assures a fine-textured bread.

• Loaves or rolls are ready to be baked when they retain the impression after being lightly touched. Glass, darkened metal, or dull-finished aluminum pans are ideal for baking bread. They absorb heat and give bread a good brown crust.

• Test bread for doneness by tapping it. It should have a hollow sound when done.

Streamlined White Bread

1 pkg. active dry yeast	3 cups all-purpose
1¼ cups warm water	flour
(not hot—110	2 tbsp. soft shortening
to 115°)	2 tsp. salt
	2 tbsp. sugar

In mixing bowl, dissolve yeast in warm water. Measure flour by dipping method (p. 123) or by sifting. Add shortening, salt, sugar, and 2 cups flour. Beat 2 min. medium speed on mixer or 300 vigorous strokes by hand. Scrape sides and bottom of bowl frequently. Add remaining flour and blend in with spoon until smooth. Scrape batter from sides of bowl. Cover with cloth and let rise in warm place (85°) until double, about 30 min.

Stir down batter by beating about 25 strokes. Spread batter evenly in greased loaf pan, 8½ x 4½ x 2¾″ or 9x5x3″. Batter will be sticky. Smooth out top of loaf by flouring hand and patting.

Let rise in warm place (85°) until batter is ¼″ from top of 8½″ pan or 1″ from top of 9″ pan, about 40 min.

Heat oven to 375° (quick mod.). Bake 45 to 50 min., or until done. To test loaf, tap the top crust; it should sound hollow. Immediately remove from pan. Place on cooling rack or across bread pans. Brush top with melted butter or shortening. Do not place in direct draft. Cool before cutting; use saw-tooth knife.

Herb Bread

Follow recipe and directions for Streamlined White Bread (above)—except with first addition of flour, add 1 tsp. caraway seeds, ½ tsp. nutmeg, and ½ tsp. crumbled or powdered sage.

Herb Bread (p. 124)

Corn Sticks (p. 80)

Caraway Bread Sticks (p. 39)

Dark Date Nut Bread (p. 11)

Anadama Loaves (p. 24)

Extra-quick Butter Sticks (p. 118)

Helpful Hints for Pastry

• Use a pastry blender for cutting the shortening into flour. The particles formed will flatten during the rolling out and thus provide the tenderness and flakiness characteristic of good pastry. A fork or spoon should not be used because it "creams" or blends rather than cuts.
• Use cold water—it will keep the shortening from melting.
• Add just enough water to moisten flour. If dough is sticky, too much flour has to be added during rolling. This toughens the pastry.
• Use a pastry set or cloth-covered board and stockinet-covered rolling pin. The flour rubbed into the cloth prevents sticking without adding too much to the pastry.
• Handle as little as possible. Rerolling and overhandling toughens pastry.

QUICK PASTRY

Just follow pkg. directions on pie crust mix.

Tender-flaky Pastry

FOR 8″ ONE-CRUST PIE	FOR 8″ TWO-CRUST PIE
1 cup all-purpose flour	1½ cups all-purpose flour
½ tsp. salt	¾ tsp. salt
⅓ cup plus 1 tbsp. shortening	½ cup plus 2 tbsp. shortening
2 tbsp. water	3 tbsp. water

Combine flour and salt in mixing bowl.

With pastry blender or 2 knives, cut in shortening until little balls about the size of peas are formed.

Sprinkle water onto flour, one tbsp. at a time. Mix lightly with fork until all flour is moistened.

Gather dough together with fingers so it cleans the bowl. Press firmly into a ball. (Divide dough for two-crust pie into 2 equal balls.)

Flatten with hand on lightly floured cloth-covered board. Roll out ⅛″ thick with stockinet-covered rolling pin. Roll lightly in all directions, keeping edge of pastry round. Pinch broken edges together immediately.

Make sure that pastry is 1″ larger all around than inverted pie pan to allow for depth of pie pan.

Fold pastry in half, and carefully transfer to pan. Ease pastry into pan. Be careful not to stretch it; stretching causes shrinkage.

Complete pie shell according to one of the three methods on p. 127.

Baking a Pie Shell

For pies that have fillings cooked separately on top of the range, such as cream-type fillings, or fillings that require no cooking, such as refrigerated fillings.

Follow recipe and directions for Pastry (p. 126). Trim pastry ½″ from edge of pan. Fold pastry under, even with pan. Flute or crimp edge.

Prick the pie shell all over with a fork so that air trapped below the shell can escape rather than cause bubbles in the crust.

Bake at 475° (very hot) 8 to 10 min.

Baking a One-crust Pie

For custard-type pies, streusel-topped pies, or pies topped with pastry cut-outs (fancy shapes cut from extra pastry).

Follow recipe and directions for Pastry (p. 126). Trim pastry ½″ from edge of pan. Fold pastry under, even with pan. Flute or crimp edge. Do not prick!

Fill and bake according to recipe.

Baking a Two-crust Pie

Generally for fruit pies.

Follow recipe and directions for Pastry (p. 126). Prepare filling of your choice. Place filling in pie and trim overhanging edges of pastry.

Roll out dough for top crust large enough to extend 1″ beyond edge of pan.

Fold pastry for top crust in half. Make slits near center to allow steam to escape during baking and prevent puffing and a soggy top crust.

Moisten edge of bottom pastry with water. Place folded pastry evenly on filling. Unfold. Trim pastry ½″ beyond edge of pan.

Fold edge of top pastry under lower pastry. Seal by pressing together with fingers on edge of pan.

Make simple edge by pressing all around with tines of fork, or fluted edge by pinching all around between thumb and forefinger.

To prevent edge from browning too rapidly, cover with 1½″ strip of aluminum foil or damp cloth before baking. Remove 15 min. before end of baking.

Bake according to recipe.

Before You Bake

1. Read the entire recipe, both ingredients and method.
2. Preheat oven to correct temperature.
3. Assemble ingredients. Have shortening, eggs, and milk at room temperature—except in hot weather when it's best to use eggs and milk directly from refrigerator.
4. Assemble utensils:
   standard measuring cups and spoons
   bowls
   spatula or rubber scraper
   wooden spoons
   electric mixer, if using it
   baking pan (Shiny aluminum pans are best for cakes. Be sure you have exact size called for in recipe.)

Brown Beauty Cake

2 sq. unsweetened chocolate (2 oz.), cut up	½ tsp. soda
	½ tsp. salt
½ cup boiling water	¼ cup soft shortening
1 cup cake flour	⅓ cup buttermilk
1 cup sugar	½ tsp. vanilla
¼ tsp. baking powder	1 egg

Heat oven to 350° (mod.). Grease and flour a square pan, 8x8x2".

Stir chocolate and boiling water until chocolate melts. Cool.

Spoon flour to overflowing into nested dry measuring cup and level off with straight-edged spatula, or sift if you wish. Blend flour, sugar, baking powder, soda, and salt. Stir into chocolate mixture.

Add shortening. Beat 1 min. medium speed on mixer or 150 vigorous strokes by hand. Scrape sides and bottom of bowl constantly. Add remaining ingredients. Beat 1 more min., scraping bowl frequently.

Pour into prepared pan. Bake 35 to 40 min. or until cake tests done. Cool. Frost with your favorite chocolate frosting.

New Starlight Cake

2 cups all-purpose flour	½ cup soft shortening
1½ cups sugar	1 cup milk
3½ tsp. baking powder	1 tsp. vanilla
1 tsp. salt	3 eggs (½ to ⅔ cup)

Heat oven to 350° (mod.). Grease and flour 2 round layer pans, 8 or 9x1½", or an oblong pan, 13x9½x2". Measure flour by dipping method (p. 123) or by sifting. Stir flour, sugar, baking powder, and salt in bowl. Add shortening, milk, and vanilla. Beat 2 min. at medium speed on mixer or 300 vigorous strokes by hand. Scrape sides and bottom of bowl constantly. Add eggs. Beat 2 more min., scraping bowl frequently. Pour into prepared pans. Bake layers 30 to 35 min., oblong 40 to 45 min. Do not underbake! Cake is done when toothpick stuck into center comes out clean. Frost as desired.

How to Use a Cake Mix for Two

To use angel food cake mix: Prepare batter for any flavor angel food cake mix. Bake cake as directed on pkg. in two loaf pans, 9x5x3". Use one cake; wrap the other in foil and freeze for another time.

To use layer cake mix: Prepare batter for any flavor layer cake mix. Use half the batter to fill 6 greased and floured miniature loaf pans, 4¾x2⅝x1½", filling each half full. Pour other half of batter into greased and floured round layer pan, 9x1½" or square pan, 8x8x2". Bake in 350° (mod.) oven: small loaves 20 to 25 min.; layer 30 to 35 min. Freeze extra loaves or layer. Loaves are excellent served sundae-style, shortcake-style, or filled and topped with sweetened whipped cream.

After You Bake

1. First, make sure your cake is done. When minimum baking time is up, touch center of top surface lightly. If no imprint remains, cake is done. An extra test for doneness is to insert a toothpick into center. If it comes out clean, cake is done.
2. Cool cake thoroughly. Leave in pan and set on wire cake rack to let air circulate around it. Let stand in pan 10 min. Turn out on towel by first putting a towel over cake, then an inverted wire cake rack over towel. Turn whole thing upside down. Lift off pan. Put another inverted rack over bottom of cake and turn again. When cool, frost with favorite icing.

Use the Right Coffee Maker in the Right Way

Choose a coffee maker that brews just the number of cups the two of you will drink at one meal. Coffee won't be as delicious if you make less than the capacity of the pot. The directions below are for non-electric coffee makers. If you have an electric coffee maker, follow the manufacturer's directions.

To Use a Dripolator: Preheat lower section by rinsing with hot water. Measure drip grind coffee into filter section. Pour freshly-boiled water into upper section. (Water will drip through grounds into lower section.) Remove sections; serve immediately.

Filter papers make the coffee extra clear. They fit exactly over the bottom of the filter section. Buy them where coffee pots are sold; store them next to the coffee so you'll be sure to use them.

To Use a Percolator: Measure fresh cold water into the pot. Measure regular grind coffee into basket. Place over heat and bring water to boil. (The steam formed will force the water up through the tube and spray it over the ground coffee; it will then drip back into the lower section. This process is called percolating.) Lower heat and percolate gently 5 to 10 min. Remove basket and serve immediately.

To Use a Vacuum Coffee Maker: Measure fresh cold water into lower bowl. Fit top bowl on with filter adjusted. Put coffee (drip grind) in top. Place on heat. When water rises, lower heat. Stir once. Remove from heat after 1 min. When coffee is back in lower section, remove top, put on separate cover. Serve immediately.

To Make Boiled Coffee: Measure regular grind coffee and fresh cold water into enamelware pot; use 2 level tbsp. coffee and ¾ cup water for each serving. Place over heat. Stir. Bring just to boil. Stir again. Take off heat. Add dash of cold water. Let grounds settle. If you have a strainer, serve coffee through strainer.

Use the Right Coffee in the Right Amount

For a Dripolator: Drip grind.

For a Percolator and Vacuum Type: Regular or percolator grind.

For medium strength, use 2 level tbsp. per coffee cup (¾ measuring cup, or 6 oz.). Suit your coffee taste by adjusting the amount of coffee you use. You may need more coffee per cup for a dripolator because the water has only one contact with the coffee. Don't try to reuse coffee grounds or prolong the brewing time. This extracts the caffeine, giving a bitter taste.

For Freshest Flavor

Buy only the amount of coffee you will use in 1 week. Store it tightly covered in a cool place.

If Coffee Must Wait

Or when making more than one potful for company:
- Keep it hot on an asbestos pad over very low heat.
- Pour it into coffee bottle or carafe and keep hot over candle flame.
- Pour into a vacuum bottle.

Warning: Watch closely! Coffee loses flavor if allowed to boil or stand indefinitely.

Freeze leftover coffee in an ice cube tray . . . when used to chill iced coffee, the ice cubes won't dilute the coffee.

Suds Away Stains

Stains in a coffee maker can ruin coffee flavor. So wash your coffee maker with hot sudsy soap and water after each use. If your coffee maker does become stained, clean according to manufacturer's directions. Boiling water with soda works beautifully for some pots; for others, a powdered coffee stain remover is necessary.

Marketing

Good marketing is just as important as good cooking—in fact, they go hand in hand because ingredients are an important part of the success of every recipe. Here's how to shorten your shopping time yet keep a well-stocked cupboard and refrigerator, ready for every occasion. Consult the charts for help in selecting the best fresh fruits and vegetables, meats, poultry, fish, and seafood.

For Easier Marketing

- Outline meal plans generally for the coming week.
- Then list the staples and extras that will be needed. (Check refrigerator and cupboards.)
- Classify and relist items to avoid retracing steps in the market.
- Plan to shop when stores are least crowded.
- Shop weekly for staples, twice weekly for perishable fruits, vegetables, and meats.
- Buy only what you can store easily and use without waste. The "large economy" or family sizes are not practical for two.
- Read labels carefully; they give valuable information.
- Put food away promptly, storing as directed.

Staples

Flour
Sugar: granulated, brown, and confectioners'
Shortening
Vinegar and oil
Salt and pepper
Baking powder and soda
Coffee, tea, cocoa, and chocolate
Cereals: ready-to-eat and hot
Macaroni, spaghetti, noodles, and rice
Prepared salad dressing
Vanilla, lemon, mint, sherry, almond extracts

Seasonings

Cinnamon
Nutmeg
Celery seeds
Garlic, celery, and onion salts
Curry powder
Chili powder
Bouillon cubes
Worcestershire sauce
Cheeses

Frozen Foods

Complete meals: poultry, meat, or sea food main dishes, appetizers, and desserts
Main dishes: pizza, chow mein
Potatoes: French fried, patties
Soups: look for new, unusual flavors
Baked cakes and pies
Pies: fruit-filled ready-to-bake; small pies for two; cream pies to thaw and serve
Extra specials: melon balls, waffle squares
Ice cream, sherbet
Berries, fruits, vegetables, fruit juices

For the Emergency Shelf

All sorts of delicious meals-in-minutes come straight off the cupboard shelf that is stocked with ever-ready foods like these. Group together all ingredients for several complete "quickie" meals, and replace items as you use them. With such a shelf and a little imagination, you are ready for all the moments when a change of plans, a problem of time, or unexpected dinner guests might—but won't—take you by surprise!

Canned Foods

Meats and fish: ham, chipped beef, corned beef, hash, luncheon meats, bacon, chicken fricassee or à la king, sardines, shrimp, lobster, crabmeat, tuna, salmon

Soups: chicken, mushroom, consommé, tomato, etc.

Whole tomatoes, tomato sauce, tomato paste

Vegetables: tiny whole cooked onions and potatoes, mushrooms, baked beans, and other favorites

Fruits: peaches, pears, fruits for salad, pineapple, apricots, fruit pie fillings

Relishes: jam, jelly, olives, pickles

Milk: evaporated or condensed

Packaged Foods

Convenience mixes: all-purpose biscuit mix, pancake mix, cooky mixes, pastry mix, cake and frosting mixes, gingerbread mix, muffin mix, pudding and pie filling mixes, fruit-flavored gelatin, dehydrated soup mixes, noodles, macaroni, rice mixes, instant mashed potatoes.

Instant beverages: coffee, tea, cocoa, bouillon cubes (chicken, beef, vegetable)

Non-fat dry milk

Grated cheese

Instant minced onion

Refrigerated Foods

Ready-to-bake biscuits and cookies (be sure to watch expiration dates)

Pizza

Whipped cream in a can

How to Select and Store Meat

How to Select

All meats, except pork, should bear the purple stamp "Prime," "Choice," "Good," "Commercial," or "Utility," as graded by the United States Department of Agriculture. Fresh pork is fairly uniform in quality and is seldom graded. Look for the round purple inspection stamp (U. S. Inspected and Passed), indicating government inspected meat.

How to Store

To store fresh meat: remove market wrapping and re-wrap in waxed paper or aluminum foil; store in coldest part of refrigerator. If meat is not to be used within three days, wrap and freeze. Ground meat and variety meats (such as liver) do not keep as well as whole cuts and should be frozen if not cooked within 24 hours.

TYPE	HOW TO CHOOSE	AMOUNT TO BUY
Beef	High quality meat has smooth, brittle, white fat; flesh of younger animals is pinkish red, while that of older animals is a deeper red.	
Roast (see p. 20 for cuts)	Select "Choice", "Good", or "Top Grade Commercial".	3 to 4 lb.
Pot Roast	May choose "Good" or "Top Grade Commercial" since meat will have slow, moist cooking. Choose blade cut, round bone, rump, or sirloin tip.	2 lb. (enough for two meals and sandwiches)
Steak	For the different cuts, see p. 59.	⅓ to ¾ lb. per serving
Liver	Should be a deep reddish-brown — never gray. Moist, shiny, fresh.	½ lb.
Ground Beef	For hamburgers, buy ground chuck which is well marbled with fat for flavor and juiciness, yet is attractively low-priced. Regular ground beef contains 25% fat; lean ground beef contains 15% fat. If you order ground round steak, ask your meat dealer to add 2 oz. of suet before grinding.	½ to 3 lb.
Veal	High quality veal has pink, solid flesh with no marbling and a very small amount of clear, firm, white fat. Veal is simply young beef; all cuts are similar though smaller.	
Chops	Choose loin or rib, 1″ thick.	1 per serving.
Cutlets	A popular cut to bread and pan-fry.	
Roast	The leg and the boned and stuffed shoulder both make excellent roasts. Since veal has so little fat, ask your meat dealer to lard the roast for you to keep it from drying out in cooking.	2 to 2½ lb.
Pork	Young pork of high quality is pinkish gray; older pork is a delicate rose color. Lean pork should be well marbled with fat, firm, and fine grained, covered by layer of fairly firm white fat.	
Chops	Loin or rib; order to thickness you prefer.	As many as you'll eat.
Tenderloin	Cut in patties and Frenched or flattened.	½ to ¾ lb.
Roast	Loin end roast includes enough meat for 2 or 3 meals. Roast the whole cut at once and use cooked meat in dishes like chow mein. Or cut out the tenderloin, flatten and fry later.	3 to 4 lb.
Spareribs	Meaty; choose regular or loin.	2 lb.
Ham	Center slice. For baked ham for two, choose a small canned ham.	½″ slices (¾ to 1 lb.)
Lamb	The flesh of good lamb is pinkish-red in young animals, deeper red in older animals.	
Chops	Loin and rib chops are more expensive and meatier, but shoulder chops are delicious when cooked to tenderness and are easy on the budget.	As many as you'll eat.
Roast	Boned sirloin roast from the leg is the best. If you are buying a whole leg of lamb or the loin half, ask to have several chops removed for another meal.	2 to 3½ lb. (enough for two meals).
Stew	Order economical cuts like shank, breast, or neck, cut up. Also excellent braised.	1 lb.
Ground Lamb	Prepare like ground beef.	½ to 1 lb.

How to Select and Store Poultry

How to Select

Poultry, whether purchased fresh or frozen, should bear packers brand name, weight, price, and USDA inspected and passed seal.

How to Store

Store fresh poultry in refrigerator; use within two days. Store frozen poultry in freezer; date the label and use within 6 months. Thaw frozen poultry completely before cooking: either unwrapped in refrigerator overnight or unwrapped in cold water 1 to 2 hr., until meat is pliable.

TYPE	HOW TO CHOOSE	AMOUNT TO BUY
Chicken		
For Roasting	Plan ¾ lb. ready-to-cook weight per serving plus cooked meat for another meal.	3 to 4 lb. roaster or 2 to 2½ lb. broiler-fryer
For Pan-frying or Oven-frying	Choose quartered or cut up broiler-fryer. If your fryer weighs just 1½ lb., fry all of it. If it's nearer 3 lb., save breasts to cook separately.	1½ to 3 lb.
For Stewing	Try to find a chicken that is meaty, not too fat. Stewing chickens are hard to find in some localities; if so, select a heavy roaster or broiler-fryer.	3½ to 5 lb.
Turkey	Allow ½ to ¾ lb. ready-to-cook weight per serving plus a generous amount as planned-over.	4 to 6 lb.

How to Select and Store Fish and Seafood

How to Select

Fresh, high-quality fish has firm, elastic flesh and no strong odor. Buy from a fish dealer who displays the fish on ice or in a freezer.

How to Store

Refrigerate fish and seafood and use within 2 days. If frozen, thaw unwrapped overnight in refrigerator or unwrapped in cold water 1 to 2 hr., or follow package directions.

TYPE	HOW TO CHOOSE	AMOUNT TO BUY
Fish	Have fish cleaned, leaving head and tail on.	1½ to 2 lb.
Fillets	Ask your fish dealer about best fish for fillets for the locality and season.	½ to ¾ lb.
Steaks	These cross-wise slices of large dressed fish are excellent broiled or baked.	¾ to 1 lb.
Seafood		
Lobster Tails	If tails are very small, serve two each.	Two 8-oz. tails
Oysters	Fresh oysters are sold only during months whose names include the letter "R".	1 pint
Shrimp	Large shrimp are easier to clean, more attractive when served, usually more expensive.	1 lb.

Meat Cookery

Every grade and cut of meat can be made tender and palatable by following certain cookery guides. These guides are: (1) the basic rules for meat cookery, (2) the control of temperature in cooking, and (3) the specific methods for cooking meat.

Basic Rules for Meat Cookery

Meat cuts are tender or less tender according to their location in the animal, the grade of meat, the amount of aging they have undergone after slaughter (applies especially to beef), and the age of the animal. In most cases the tenderness of a meat cut determines the method or methods which may be used for cooking it. Certain cookery methods are adapted to the tender cuts, while others are especially suited to the less tender cuts.

In general, tender cuts are best when cooked by dry heat methods, such as roasting, broiling, pan-broiling, and frying. On the other hand, less tender cuts are made tender by cooking with moist heat, such as braising and cooking in liquid where meat is surrounded by either steam or hot liquid. It requires long slow cooking in moisture to soften connective tissue—the part of meat which may not be tender. Braising is the method by which pot roasts and Swiss steaks are cooked. Large cuts and stews are cooked in liquid.

There are a few exceptions to the general rule of dry heat for tender and moist heat for less tender cuts. Some thin cuts of meat, such as chops, steaks, and cutlets of pork and veal, need to be well done. They are better when braised or fried, rather than broiled or pan-broiled. Braising or pan-frying cooks them well done without drying them out.

Cooking Temperature

Meat is a much better product when it is cooked slowly—more tender, juicier, and more flavorful; it is also more uniformly cooked. Then too, 15 to 20% of meat shrinkage can be prevented by the use of low temperatures.

Cooking time is only an approximate guide to the degree of doneness. Many factors affect the cooking time, such as (1) the cooking temperature, (2) the size and shape of the cut, (3) the grade of meat, and (4) the amount of aging. Only beef of high quality, however, is aged.

The meat thermometer is the most accurate guide to the degree of doneness, especially of roasts. In other words the internal temperature of meat indicates its degree of doneness.

Specific Methods for Cooking Meat

There are six specific methods for cooking meat. The dry heat methods are: roasting, broiling, pan-broiling, and frying. Moist heat methods are: braising and cooking in liquid.

How to Roast

1. Season with salt and pepper, if desired.
2. Place meat, fat side up, on rack in roasting pan.
3. Insert a meat thermometer so that bulb is in center of largest muscle.
4. Do not add water, do not cover.
5. Roast at 325° (except fresh pork, 350°) until done.

How to Broil

1. Turn oven regulator to "broil."
2. Place meat on rack of broiler pan 2 or 3 inches from heat.
3. Broil until top side is brown.
4. Season top side with salt and pepper.
5. Turn and brown on the other side.
6. Season and serve at once.

How to Pan-broil

1. Place meat in heavy frying pan.
2. Cook slowly.
3. Do not add fat or water.
4. Turn occasionally.
5. Pour off excess fat.
6. Brown meat on both sides.
7. Do not overcook. Season and serve at once.

How to Pan-fry

1. Use a heavy frying pan.
2. Brown meat on both sides in a small amount of fat.
3. Season or coat with Seasoned Flour: 1 cup all-purpose flour, 2 tsp. salt, ¼ tsp. pepper, ½ tsp. celery salt, ¼ tsp. paprika.
4. Do not cover meat.
5. Cook at moderate temperature until done. Turn occasionally.

How to Braise

1. Brown meat slowly on all sides in heavy skillet.
2. Season with salt and pepper.
3. Add a small amount of liquid.
4. Cover tightly; cook at a low temperature until tender.

How to Cook in Liquid (Stews)

1. Cut meat in uniform pieces, one- to two-inch cubes.
2. If a brown stew is required, brown meat on all sides.
3. Add just enough water or soup stock to cover the meat. Cover kettle and *simmer* until tender. Do not boil.
4. Add vegetables to the meat at the proper time so as not to overcook them.

How to Select Vegetables

Quality vegetables are well shaped, clean, bright in color, free of spots or bruises.

How to Store Vegetables

Store potatoes and onions in a cool dark place. Store other vegetables in the refrigerator in a plastic bag or hydrator.

TYPE	AMOUNT TO BUY
Asparagus	1 lb.
Beans (Green, Wax, or Snap)	½ to ¾ lb.
Broccoli	¾ lb.
Brussels sprouts	½ to ¾ lb.
Cabbage (Green, Red, or Chinese)	1 small head (2 cups shredded serves two)
Carrots	1 bunch (5 or 6 medium serves two)
Cauliflower	1 small head (½ head serves two)
Celery, diced	1 bunch (1 to 1½ cups cut up serves two)
Corn on the Cob	4 ears
Lima beans	1½ lb. in pod (1 cup shelled)
Onions	2 to 3 lb. (¾ lb. serves two)
Peas	1½ lb. in pod (1 cup shelled)
Potatoes (White or Sweet)	5 lb. (1 lb. serves two)
Squash: Winter (such as Acorn or Hubbard)	1 lb.
Summer (Green or Yellow)	1 lb.

Hints on Vegetables

To find directions for cooking individual vegetables, look up the vegetable in the index.
• Cook *green* vegetables 10 to 20 minutes or just until crisp-tender. Cook uncovered for the first 5 minutes to preserve chlorophyll and color. Then cover and finish cooking.
• Add 1 tsp. vinegar to *red cabbage* near end of cooking time to preserve red color.
• Cook *yellow* vegetables, covered, in small amount of water for shortest possible time, until just tender.
• Cook strong-flavored vegetables, such as cauliflower, uncovered in large amount of water to prevent strong odor and flavor.
• For two, buy 1 pkg. frozen vegetables or 8-oz. can. Try several brands, then choose the best quality in your price range.
• Keep frozen vegetables in refrigerator freezing compartment until cooking time. Do not thaw.
• Save stock from cooking vegetables for use in soups.
• Vegetables may be boiled, baked, or sautéed.

How to Select Greens

Choose a heavy head of lettuce for tossed salads; for lettuce cups, choose a lighter one. When choosing other greens, such as leaf lettuce, look for leaves that are firm, crisp, and free of spots or rust streaks.

How to Store Greens

Refrigerate. Wash thoroughly before using. For really crisp salad greens, wash and dry them early in the day and refrigerate in plastic bag or hydrator.

TYPE	AMOUNT TO BUY
Head lettuce	1 head makes 5 servings of salad
Leaf lettuce, escarole, curly endive, French endive, romaine, chicory, spinach, Boston lettuce, watercress	1 pkg. or bunch

Meats and "Go-With" Vegetables

Beef—broccoli, cabbage, cauliflower, celery, green beans, tomatoes, beets, mushrooms, eggplant, white turnips, parsnips, kohlrabi.

Chicken—corn, Lima beans, peas, sweet potatoes.

Fish—tomatoes, peas, green beans, asparagus, cucumbers, celery.

Ham—asparagus, broccoli, Brussels sprouts, celery, green beans, cabbage, cauliflower, spinach and other greens, zucchini.

Lamb—artichokes (French), carrots, peas, winter squash, creamed cauliflower, yellow turnips.

Pork—cabbage, cauliflower, celery, spinach and other greens, tomatoes, summer squash.

Turkey—creamed onions, mashed rutabagas, Hubbard squash, sweet potatoes, Brussels sprouts.

Veal—artichokes (French), beets, creamed asparagus, fried eggplant, succotash, winter squash, creamed mushrooms.

FRUITS	HOW TO CHOOSE	HOW MUCH TO BUY	HOW TO STORE
Apples *For eating:* Delicious McIntosh Winesap Northern Spy *For cooking:* Baldwin, Greening, Rome Beauty, Winesap, Jonathan, Duchess, Wealthy	Firm, with good color, no shriveling of peel. Immature fruit lacks color and flavor.	3 to 5 lb.	In cool, dry place or refrigerator.
Avocados	Shiny, plump, green with no black spots. Skin should yield slightly to gentle pressure.	1 serves two	At room temperature.
Bananas	Uniform yellow color with brown speckles. No green showing. May be bought green and then ripened before using.	1 to 2 lb.	Do not refrigerate. Store in brown paper bag to ripen.
Cherries *For pies and cooking:* sour cherries. *For the table:* sweet or Bing cherries.	Deep red color, firm, unshriveled.	½ lb.	Refrigerate.
Melons Cantaloupe	Coarse netting on green or gray rind. Sweet, fine texture, pungent aroma. Ripe if soft near stem end.	½ to 1 serves two	Refrigerate.
Casaba	Large, round, yellow with juicy, white meat. Late variety. Blossom end of melon should be soft.		
Honeydew	Oval, smooth, whitish-green rind with green, juicy, sweet flesh. Blossom end should be slightly soft.		
Persian	Large, round, with well-defined netting on rind. Resembles cantaloupe. Deep orange-pink flesh, thick and mildly flavored. Soft at stem end.		

FRUITS	HOW TO CHOOSE	HOW MUCH TO BUY	HOW TO STORE
Melons (continued) Watermelon	Symmetrical and green in color with velvety apppearance, yellow underside. Crisp, juicy red or pink flesh. Thumps with dull hollow sound when rapped.	¼ to ½	Refrigerate.
Oranges *For slices or sections:* Navel (navel formation opposite stem end). *For juice and sections:* Valencia.	Thick, bright orange peel, seedless. Thin skin, few seeds.	½ dozen	In cool place or refrigerate.
Peaches	Round, plump, smooth with good color; medium or large size without blemishes. Avoid soft, cracked appearance. Very perishable when ripe.	2 medium peaches serve two	Refrigerate.
Pears *In July-Oct.:* Bartlett (bell shape, sweet, juicy). *In Oct.-May:* D'Anjou (green skin, fine grained).	Slightly soft when pressed near stem end; without blemishes.	2 medium pears serve two	If not quite ripe, store at room temperature until ripe. When ripe, refrigerate.
Pineapple	Top center leaves pull out easily; distinct crevices surround each section. Fruit should be pliable to touch, heavy for its size.	1 serves two	In cool place.
Rhubarb	Firm, crisp, tender pink or red. Thick stalks. Younger stems are tender and delicate. Leaves are not edible.	1 lb. for 2 cups sauce	In cool, dry place or refrigerator.
Strawberries	Bright, clear, fresh and fragrant. Medium-sized, tart, well-shaped with green caps. Highly perishable.	1 quart yields 3 cups—4 or 5 servings.	Pick over carefully, spread on tray, refrigerate. For best flavor and texture, do not wash until just before serving.

Salad Secrets

Use only well-drained fruits and vegetables and crisp dry greens—fresh, chilled, and colorful.

Plan salads to complement and harmonize with the rest of the meal—a light salad with a hearty meal, a tart salad with fish, a crisp salad with a soft-textured casserole.

Avoid repeating in a salad flavors which are included elsewhere in the meal.

Use just enough dressing to coat each ingredient lightly—too much makes salads limp or soggy.

Keep more than one kind of dressing on hand to lend variety to your salads.

Fruit Salads

Most fruit salads may be arranged and dressed well ahead of serving time and kept refrigerated while the fruit and dressing flavors blend.

To prevent peeled fresh apples, bananas, peaches, and pears from darkening, dip them in lemon, grapefruit, or orange juice, which can also serve as a simple dressing.

For special occasions, serve fruit salads dramatically in halves of melon, orange, or grapefruit, from which the meat has been removed. With a sharp knife, cut a decorative zig-zag or scalloped edge. Or serve fruits in avocado halves, pineapple boats, or glass dishes set within larger dishes of crushed ice.

Garnish fruit salads with any one of these:

- pomegranate seeds
- balls of soft yellow or cream cheese rolled in chopped nuts
- prunes or dates stuffed with cream cheese
- sherbet
- celery seeds
- poppy seeds
- mint sprigs
- lime wedges
- slivered or chopped nuts
- frosted grapes
- cottage cheese

Tossed Salads

Wash, drain, and dry salad greens. Keep them chilled and crisp in large ventilated plastic bag or hydrator in refrigerator. Leafy greens turn brown quickly if tightly packed or covered.

Create more interesting salads by using two or more kinds of greens.

Tear—do not cut—greens into easy-to-eat pieces to avoid bruising.

For a mild garlic flavor, rub the inside of a wooden salad bowl with a cut clove of garlic; then discard garlic.

Add the dressing and toss the salad at serving time; add tomatoes last to avoid diluting the dressing.

The basic dressing for a tossed salad is made in proportions of two parts olive or salad oil to one part vinegar, seasoned with salt and freshly ground black pepper. To vary this recipe, use either tarragon or wine vinegar or lemon juice. A little basil, thyme, marjoram, rosemary, oregano, or dill lends distinctive character to dressings.

Besides greens, a tossed salad may contain or be garnished with one or several of the following:

- thinly sliced radishes
- fringed cucumber slices
- green pepper rings
- onion or chives
- cut fresh green beans
- thinly sliced raw mushrooms
- cauliflowerets
- thinly sliced zucchini squash
- freshly shelled green peas
- celery curls
- green or ripe olives
- artichoke hearts
- cooked or canned vegetables
- croutons
- shredded or grated cheese—Swiss, Bleu, Cheddar, Parmesan
- julienne strips of meat or poultry
- sliced or sieved hard-cooked egg
- pickle fans
- sliced carrots

Tossed Salad (p. 140)

Tomatoes Vinaigrette (p. 73)

Asparagus Tips with Mayonnaise (p. 56)

Orange-Bermuda Onion Salad (p. 9)

Apple and Grapefruit Salad (p. 75)

Festival Peach Salad (p. 96)

What Every Kitchen

For Preparation

rolling pin and cover
pastry cloth
pastry blender
cutting board
cutlery set (butcher knife, 7 or 8″
    blade; bread knife, serrated
    blade; 2 paring knives)
strainer (med. mesh, med. size)
bottle and jar opener
can opener
colander
grater or shredder
long-handled fork
pancake turner
vegetable peeler
lemon squeezer
funnel
2 kitchen tablespoons
2 kitchen teaspoons
vegetable brush
slotted spoon
kitchen scissors
tongs
electric mixer
electric toaster

For Mixing

rotary beater
mixing bowls (convenient sizes)
large wooden spoon (11″)
rubber scraper

For Top-of-the-Range Cooking

covered frying pan (10″)
frying pan (6″)
covered saucepans (1 qt., 2 qt.,
    4 to 6 qt.)
coffee maker
teapot
teakettle
double boiler (1½ qt.)
salt and pepper shakers

for Two Needs . . .

For Baking

oblong pan (13x9½x2″)
bread loaf pan (9x5x3″)
2 square pans (8x8x2″ and
   9x9x1¾″)
baking sheet (without sides)
muffin pan (6 or 12 cups)
pie pan (8″)
3 cooling racks for cooling cakes,
   breads, cookies
baking dish with cover (1½ qt.)
6 custard cups
pot holders

For Measuring

1 set nested dry measuring cups
   (¼, ⅓, ½ and 1 cup sizes)
liquid measuring cup (1 cup size)
1 set measuring spoons (¼, ½,
   1 tsp. and 1 tbsp. sizes)
1 spatula (7″ blade)

Nice to Have

potato masher
wire whip
tube pan (10x4″ deep)
utility tray
2 round layer pans (9″)
roasting pan (with rack)
Dutch oven
pressure cooker
kitchen thermometers (meat,
   candy, fat)
food chopper or grinder with fine
   and coarse cutters
griddle
gelatin molds
ladle
jelly roll pan (15½x10½x1″)
kitchen timer
refrigerator containers
electric blender
knife sharpener
soufflé dish
melon ball cutter
garlic press
cake safe

Glossary

A

antipasto — (ahn-tee-PAHS-to) Italian for assorted appetizers of fish, cold cuts, vegetables, or relishes.

aspic — A jelly made from concentrated vegetable, meat, or fish stock . . . with gelatin.

au gratin — (awh-GRAH-tin) With a browned covering of bread crumbs, often mixed with butter or cheese.

B

bake — To cook by dry heat in oven.

barbecue — To roast meat on a grill, spit, over coals, or under a free flame or oven electric unit, usually basting with a highly seasoned sauce. The term is popularly applied to foods cooked in or served with barbecue sauce.

baste — To moisten meat or other foods while cooking to add flavor and to prevent drying of the surface. The liquid is usually melted fat, meat drippings, fruit juice, or sauce.

batter — A mixture of flour and liquid, or in combination with other ingredients, thin enough to pour; such as cake batter, pancake batter, batter used to coat foods for frying.

beat —To make a mixture smooth or to introduce air by using a brisk, regular motion that lifts the mixture over and over.

blanch — To plunge into boiling water; then in certain cases, into cold water. Nuts and fruits are blanched to remove skins easily.

blend — To combine two or more ingredients.

boil — To heat to boiling point, or heat so as to cause bubbles to break on surface.

bouillon — (BOO-yahn) A clear meat broth.

bouillon cube — A small cube of concentrated chicken, meat, or vegetable stock used with boiling water to make a broth.

braise — (brayz) A method of cooking meat in a small amount of liquid for tenderness and flavor.

bread — 1. To coat with flour, egg, and crumbs.
2. A food made of flour and liquid, kneaded and baked.

broil — To cook directly under heating unit.

C

canape — (KAN-a-pee) A bite-sized appetizer consisting of plain, toasted, or fried bread, crackers, miniature cream puffs, or small shapes of thin crisp pastry, topped with cheese, meat, or sea food.

caramelize — (KAR-a-mel-ize) To melt granulated sugar over medium heat to a golden brown syrup.

chop — To cut into fine or coarse pieces with sharp knife or chopper.

consommé — (kahn-sah-MAY) A soup made from beef, veal, and chicken and condensed by boiling . . . highly seasoned, cleared, and strained.

creole — (KREE-ohl) Well-seasoned food containing tomato, green pepper, and onion; the influence of early French and Spanish settlers of Louisiana.

croquette — (kro-KET) Finely chopped chicken or fish, mixed with seasonings and thick white sauce; shaped, coated with eggs and crumbs, and fried until crisp.

croutons — (kroo-TAHNS) Small cubes of bread, fried or toasted until crisp; to serve with soups or as a garnish.

curry — 1. A combination of approximately 16 spicy ingredients; originated in India. Available in powdered form, it is used to give characteristic flavor to stews, sauces, main dishes. 2. A dish containing curry seasoning.

cut in — To incorporate fat into flour mixture, using a pastry blender, a fork, or two knives.

cutlet — A small piece of meat, cut from leg or ribs, for broiling or frying. Or a mixture, such as fish, shaped like a meat cutlet.

—————— **D** ——————

dice — To cut into very small cubes (about ¼″).

dough — A mixture of flour and liquid in combination with other ingredients, thick enough to roll, or to drop from a spoon.

drippings — Fat and juice from meat that collect in bottom of roasting pan.

—————— **E** ——————

entrée — (AHN-tray) In formal dinners, a small "made" dish that is served as a separate course between the heavy courses. In informal meals, the chief dish of the main course . . . of meat, poultry, fish, or meat substitute.

—————— **F** ——————

filet mignon — (fe-LAY min-YAHN) Choice, thick, round slice of beef from the tenderloin, usually broiled.

fillet — (fe-LAY) Long, thin, boneless strip of lean meat or fish — usually a choice cut.

fold in — To combine by using two motions, cutting vertically through the mixture and turning over and over by sliding the implement across the bottom of the mixing bowl with each turn.

French fry — To cook in hot fat deep enough to float the food.

fricassee — (FRICK-a-see) 1. Properly, to cook by braising. 2. Dish of fowl or meat, cut into pieces and stewed in gravy . . . the browning process may be omitted.

fry — To cook in hot fat.

—————— **G** ——————

garnish — To decorate with pieces of contrasting, colorful food.

glaze — To add luster to a food by coating with a syrup or jelly.

grate — To rub against grater to shred food.

gravy, kettle — The liquid in which pot roasts and stews have been simmered, thickened with a flour and cold water mixture.

gravy, pan — The liquid made from the drippings left in the pan after cooking meats (roasts, steaks, chops, and fried chicken), to which flour and water (or meat stock, bouillon-cube broth) have been added.

grill — To cook food directly over an open fire or flaming coals.

grind — To cut or crush in a food grinder.

―――――― **H** ――――――

herbs — (erbs) Aromatic plants used for garnish and seasonings, also used medicinally. A few commonly used herbs are oregano, thyme, marjoram, basil, sage, and mint.

hors d'oeuvres — (or-DERV) Dainty pieces of hot or cold food served as appetizers. Usually colorful, varied in size and shape, and served on toothpicks.

―――――― **J** ――――――

julienne — (joo-lee-EN) To cut food into match-like strips.

―――――― **K** ――――――

knead — To work dough with a pressing motion accompanied by folding and stretching. Or to press dough with heel of hand . . . alternately folding, pushing, and stretching it.

―――――― **L** ――――――

lard — 1. To insert strips of fat into or place on top of uncooked meat before roasting for flavor and moisture. 2. Fat from pork.

leavening — An ingredient added to batter or dough for baked products to make them light and porous by releasing or forming gas during baking; baking soda, baking powder, yeast.

leek — Onion-like bulb, but smaller, more pungent than onion.

legumes — (leh-GEWM) Vegetables which bear their fruit or seeds in pods, such as peas, beans, or lentils; often dried.

―――――― **M** ――――――

marbling — Fine streaks of white fat interspersed throughout the lean muscle of high-quality beef, pork, and lamb. Veal has no marbling.

marinade — (mar-e-NAYD) An oil-acid mixture used to give flavor and sometimes to tenderize meats and vegetables.

marinate — To let food stand in oil-acid mixture for added flavor and sometimes tenderness.

meringue — (meh-RANG) A stiffly beaten mixture of egg whites and sugar (1) used to cover the top of pie, pudding, and other desserts—usually browned; (2) made into small cakes or cookies and baked; (3) made into form of shells and baked, then filled; or (4) incorporated into other desserts such as refrigerator desserts.

mince — To chop or cut into very small pieces.

monosodium glutamate (MSG) —A white crystalline substance made from vegetable proteins. Enhances natural flavor of foods.

mousse — (mooss) 1. Light airy dessert, jellied or frozen. It may contain whipped egg white, whipped cream, and/or gelatin. 2. Meat or fish mold containing gelatin, whipped egg white, and/or whipped cream.

P

pan-broil— To cook uncovered in ungreased or lightly greased hot skillet, pouring off fat as it accumulates.

pan-fry (sauté) — To cook in small amount of fat in skillet.

parboil — To cook food partially in boiling water. The cooking is then completed by another method.

pare — To cut off outside skin, as from apple or potato.

parfait —(pahr-FAY) 1. A frozen dessert of whipped cream and eggs cooked with syrup and flavoring. 2. Ice cream in tall stemmed glasses.

pasta — (PAH-sta) Dough paste as spaghetti, macaroni, etc., cooked or uncooked.

patty — A shell of puffed paste filled with a creamed mixture of chicken, fish, etc.

peel — To strip off outside covering, as from orange, banana, or tomato.

pilaf or pilau–(pee-LAHF or pee-LAW) Main dish of rice, seasonings, and meat, fish, or poultry. Far Eastern origin.

pit — To remove pits or seeds from fruit.

poach — To cook by surrounding with simmering (not boiling) water or other liquid, using care to retain shape of food.

puree — (pyoo-RAY) 1. To press fruit or vegetables through a fine sieve. 2. A smooth, thick mixture made by rubbing cooked foods through a sieve.

R

ramekin — (RAM-eken) An individual baking dish.

ravioli — (rav-ee-OHL-ee) Small shapes of Italian or noodle paste, spread with a meat or vegetable filling, folded over, and poached in meat stock or baked in tomato sauce and cheese.

relish — Fresh raw vegetables cut into a variety of shapes, usually fancy; such as carrot curls, celery sticks or curls, radish roses, fringed cucumber slices, cauliflowerets.

roast — To cook, usually meats, by dry heat . . . usually in oven, sometimes over open fire, in ashes, or on heated stones or metals.

roll — 1. To place on a board and spread thin with a rolling pin. 2. A small shape made from dough and baked.

rosette —A thin batter baked in a fancy shape by means of a special iron and served with creamed foods, fruit, or ice cream. Sometimes called a timbale case.

roux — (roo) A mixture of flour and butter used to thicken sauces and soups.

S

sauerbraten —(SOWR-braht-n) German for a pot roast which has been marinated in spiced vinegar, cooked in the marinade, and served with a gingersnap gravy.

sauté — (saw-TAY) To brown or cook in small amount of fat in skillet.

scald — To heat to temperature just below boiling point until a skin forms over the top.

scallion — A young, bulbless green onion.

schaum torte —(shawm tort) Dessert consisting of baked meringue shell or layers, served with a filling of fruit, and topped with whipped cream.

score — To cut narrow gashes part way through outer surface of food.

sear — To brown surface quickly.

shallot — A mild, aromatic, purple-hued member of the onion family. The small, pear-shaped bulb contains cloves similar to garlic.

sherbet — A frozen dessert made of fruit juice, sugar, and milk or cream.

shortening — A fat suitable for baking or frying.

shred — To tear or cut into small but long pieces.

sift — To pass through a sieve to remove lumps.

simmer — To cook in liquid just below boiling point on top of range.

skewer — 1. A long pin of wood or metal on which food is placed for cooking or used to fasten meat to keep its shape during cooking.

skim — To remove top layer of fat from liquid, such as gravy or meat broth, by sliding spoon across surface of liquid.

soufflé — (soo-FLAY) A delicate, fluffy baked dish containing cheese, minced meat, or vegetables for a main dish; fruit, chocolate, nuts, etc. for a dessert. It is made light by stiffly beaten egg whites.

spice — Any of various aromatic vegetable products (as pepper, cinnamon, nutmeg, allspice, ginger, or cloves) used in cooking to season and flavor foods.

steam — To cook in the steam which arises in a pan from boiling water or other liquid.

steep — To extract flavor, color, or other qualities from a substance by allowing it to stand in liquid just below the boiling point.

stew — To cook slowly, covered by liquid, for a long time.

stock — The liquid in which meat, poultry, fish, or vegetables have been cooked.

T

taco — (TAHK-oh) A Mexican sandwich made of a tortilla wrapped around meat, fish, beans, or other food, then fried in deep fat or baked.

tamale — (tuh-MAH-lee) A highly seasoned Mexican dish of ground meat, seasonings, cooked corn meal, beans, ripe olives, and fat, wrapped in oiled corn husks, steamed or boiled.

timbale — (TIM-bal) An unsweetened custard or white sauce combined with vegetables, meat, poultry, or fish and baked in individual molds.

timbale case — A small pastry shell fried on a timbale iron and filled with creamy food.

torte — A rich cake, usually made from crumbs, eggs, and nuts . . . or a meringue in cake form.

tortilla — (tor-TEE-yah) A thin round Mexican cake made of corn meal and hot water; baked on a griddle. Mexican hot mixtures are often wrapped in them.

toss — To mix ingredients lightly without mashing them.

W

whip — To beat rapidly to produce expansion through the incorporation of air, as in egg whites and whipping cream.

Equivalent Charts

Abbreviations Commonly Used

tsp.—teaspoon
tbsp.—tablespoon
pt.—pint
qt.—quart

pk.—peck
bu.—bushel
oz.—ounce
lb.—pound or pounds
sq.—square

min.—minute or minutes
hr.—hour or hours
mod.—moderate or moderately
doz.—dozen

Simplified Measures

dash—less than ⅛ teaspoon
3 teaspoons—1 tablespoon
16 tablespoons—1 cup

1 cup—½ pint
2 cups—1 pint
2 pints (4 cups)—1 quart
4 quarts (liquid)—1 gallon

8 quarts (solid)—1 peck
4 pecks—1 bushel
16 ounces—1 pound

If you want to measure part-cups by the tablespoon, remember:

4 tablespoons—¼ cup
5⅓ tablespoons—⅓ cup

8 tablespoons—½ cup
10⅔ tablespoons—⅔ cup

12 tablespoons—¾ cup
14 tablespoons—⅞ cup

Oven Temperatures

Slow—250 to 300°
Slow moderate—325°

Moderate—350°
Quick moderate—375°
Moderately hot—400°

Hot—425 to 450°
Very hot—475 to 500°

Contents of Cans

Of the different sizes of cans used by commercial canners, the most common are:

Size	Approximate Weight	Average Contents
8 oz.	8 oz.	1 cup
picnic	10½ to 12 oz.	1¼ cups
no. 300	14 to 16 oz.	1¾ cups
no. 1 tall	1 lb.	2 cups
no. 303	16 to 17 oz.	2 cups
no. 2	1 lb. 4 oz. *or* 1 pt. 2 fl. oz.	2½ cups
no. 2½	1 lb. 13 oz.	3½ cups
no. 3	3 lb. 3 oz. *or* 1 qt. 14 fl. oz.	5¾ cups
no. 10	6½ lb. to 7 lb. 5 oz.	12 to 13 cups

Index